CAPE COD

A N D   T H E

CIVIL WAR

THE RAISED RIGHT ARM

STAUFFER MILLER

Charleston   London

THE
History
PRESS

Published by The History Press
Charleston, SC 29403
www.historypress.net

Front cover: Top, left to right: Alvin Fish, *U.S. Army Heritage and Education Center;* George Wartrous,
Harwich Historical Society; Andrew T. Shiverick, *Woods Hole Historical Collection. Bottom:* Forty-first
Massachusetts Regiment, *University of Virginia Special Collections.*
Back cover: Top: Band of Fifty-sixth Massachusetts Regiment, *U.S. Army Heritage and Education Center;*
Inset: Sidney Brooks, Harwich Historical Society.

First published 2010

Manufactured in the United States
ISBN 978.1.59629.984.9
Library of Congress Cataloging-in-Publication Data
Miller, Stauffer.
Cape Cod in the Civil War : the raised right arm / Stauffer Miller.
p. cm.
Includes bibliographical references and index.
ISBN 978-1-59629-984-9
1. Cape Cod (Mass.)--History--19th century. 2. Massachusetts--History--Civil War, 1861-
1865. 3. United States--History--Civil War, 1861-1865. 4. Cape Cod (Mass.)--Biography. 5.
Massachusetts--History--Civil War, 1861-1865--Biography. 6. United States--History--Civil
War, 1861-1865--Biography. I. Title.
F72.C3M64 2010
974.4'9203--dc22
2010037822

CONTENTS

Maps   5

Acknowledgements   7

Introduction   9

1. Abolition and Politics   11

2. First Blood   25

3. Cape Cod and the Navy   35

4. The Transports   43

5. Home Front and Front Line, 1861–62   53

6. Home Front and Front Line, 1863   75

7. Home Front and Front Line, 1864–65   85

8. Final Trumpet   105

Appendix A: Cape Cod Civil War Transport Personnel   109

Appendix B: Cape Cod Civil War Officers   117

Appendix C: Cape Cod Civil War Deaths   121

Notes   135

Bibliography   145

Index   149

About the Author   159

MAPS

Cape Cod (Barnstable County), circa 1860   12
Civil War North Carolina   42
Sandwich, circa 1860   60
Battle of Glendale, Virginia, June 30, 1862   73
Civil War Virginia, 1864   88
Battle of Spotsylvania, May 12, 1864   90

ACKNOWLEDGEMENTS

S o many people assisted me in this project that it would be best to call it a collaborative effort. Chief collaborators were my computer team of wife Ellie, friend Susan Hanson and editor Jeff Saraceno. Ellie helped me turn my computer from master into slave and exploit its great powers of information organization, storage and retrieval. Susan, of Wisconsin and daughter of solid Truro stock, mined the Internet and her mind, unearthing countless valuable nuggets. Jeff patiently guided me down the dpi highway to extract the highest-quality images possible from the rather questionable graphics I presented to him.

To write about Civil War-era Cape Cod, one must reckon with the great importance of Sandwich. There to help me with that place was Barbara Gill of its town archives. One especially fine piece of information she found was that soldier Samuel Wood was Native American. She also forwarded copies of the useful George Haines letters. Jim Coogan of Sandwich answered queries about Quakers. Helping with Falmouth matters were Mary Sicchio of Cape Cod Community College, Susan Witzell of Woods Hole Historical Society and the reference librarians at Falmouth Library, who graciously sent me *Falmouth Enterprise* articles. Joyce Peay of Falmouth and the Cape Cod Genealogical Society illuminated me on the operation of the substitute system.

Indispensable were the online issues of *The Barnstable Patriot*, placed there through the grant-writing capabilities of Lucy Loomis, director of Sturgis Library in Barnstable Village. Barnstable town clerk Linda Hutchenrider kindly shared the elegant Barnstable Rebellion Record book. Jim Gould of Cotuit lent assistance with the soldiers of Marstons Mills; Eva Needs of Centerville helped with her ancestral family, the Holways; and Burton Derick of Dennis provided a copied diary of Francis Cahoon of Chatham and other useful materials. Kathleen Remillard, adult services librarian at Brewster Ladies Library, forwarded useful items. Sally Leighton, also of Brewster, found and photographed gravestones. Ellen St. Sure furnished assistance with the Crosby's of Brewster. Responding to every request was Desiree Mobed, director of the Harwich Historical Society. Margery Campbell of East Harwich answered genealogical questions.

While surfing the Web, I came across Paul Badger of Orleans. Not only did he encourage me to research his ancestor Aaron Snow but he worked with Mary Ann Gray of the Chatham Historical Society to get me a copy of the Francis Rogers diary. Furthermore, through work with Roberta Cornish at the Eastham Historical Society, he put me on the track of the diaries of Joseph J. Rudolph and Nathan Gill. Bonnie Snow was her usual helpful self with inquiries relating to Orleans. Cynthia Moore photographed gravestones and scanned newspaper images. Off-cape, Laura Pereira of the New Bedford Whaling Museum located for me the Maria W. Jones Diary; Mark Savolis of Worcester explained the workings of Civil War artillery; and Jennifer Fauxsmith alerted me to the excellent executive letters series at Massachusetts State Archives.

Further afield, Elizabeth Margutti of the University of Virginia's Alderman Library found obscure but invaluable government documents. Terry Reimer at the National Civil War Medicine Museum in Frederick, Maryland, answered several questions. Jill D'Andrea of the National Archives in Washington helped me through the process of first knowing what to request from its vast holdings and then making the request. Marjorie McNinch of the Hagley Library in Delaware provided photocopies of Du Pont letters. Bob Shea of Atkinson, New Hampshire, contributed ideas and corrected my mistakes in ship terminology. Mike Garabedian of Wardman Library of Whittier College in California furnished a copy of a pertinent Parker Pillsbury letter.

I am dedicating this book to Dick Jurkowski of Marstons Mills, who died unexpectedly and prematurely in October 2009. He was always supportive of me and interested in what I was doing. What more can be asked of a friend? One great bond we shared was our passion for the New England Patriots football team, which brings to mind some lines of sports writer Grantland Rice: "For when the One Great Scorer comes to mark against your name, He writes—not that you won or lost—but how you played the game." Dick played the game with humor, goodwill and integrity.

INTRODUCTION

War and earthquakes are similar. Both are characterized by a prolonged buildup of stress—above ground with war and below with the earthquake—until pressures become so great that it is uncontainable, and a violent, cataclysmic eruption occurs. Through the decades of the 1830s, '40s and '50s, stress between America's Northern and Southern sections built to the point that war erupted in 1861. These two intervals or time periods—the stress and the eruption—constituted America and Cape Cod's era of the Civil War.

Working on the fault line of the rumbling slavery issue were the numerous Cape Cod ship captains trading with Southern ports. With enactment of the Fugitive Slave Law in 1850, they became bound by law to uphold it; that is, prevent the release of any fugitive slave found on board and see to his return South. Sympathy for the slave or slavery cause mattered not. Heavy fines and even imprisonment came with failure to comply. Pulled one way by the preaching of the abolitionists and their sense of humanity and the other by law and a desire to maintain livelihoods and good relations in Charleston, Savannah and Mobile, the Cape captains did their jobs and, for the most part, kept their own counsel.

Considering the Cape's pocketbook interest in a healthy Southern trade, conventional wisdom would say it would vote in support of the Democrats, the party of placating the South. However, in a seeming contradiction, in the presidential elections of 1856 and 1860, it overwhelmingly favored the Republicans—the party that, if elected, would most likely divide the country and disrupt that trade. But radically Republican the Cape people were not. When abolitionist John Brown attempted to incite slaves to rebellion, a huge gathering of Cape citizens condemned his actions. All that can be concluded is that, as Cape Cod moved through midcentury, its political stances were a confusingly contradictory mix of liberality and conservatism.

With seismic force, the war broke out. Men from the Cape went South to serve, with more than 1,000 serving in the army alone. Sandwich, with a large land-based labor force because of numerous water- and wood-powered mills and factories, furnished the most. In another seeming contradiction, men of the Cape favored the army over the navy, despite the large maritime base. The latter resource did not go untapped, however, as substantial numbers of Cape seamen served in the Union navy and the government transport service.

The people of the Cape were enormously interested in their men at war, since, in many cases, they were extensions of their own communities. For instance, the Thirty-eighth Massachusetts Regiment was a little piece of Falmouth down in Louisiana. Likewise, the men at the front wanted to know the goings-on at home. Charles Chipman of Sandwich welcomed mailings of the Sandwich's *Cape Cod Advocate* newspaper and John J. Ryder of Brewster those of the *Yarmouth Register.* Thomas Gibbs asked his mother what was "about" in Pocasset. Joshua Gould of Orleans scolded his for not sending letters.

Most Cape soldiers did their duty without incident. A few were rascals, rogues and, yes, residents of the guardhouse. Some were at the epicenter of the earthquake that was the war; others were at the periphery. This is the story of those men, their families, the people and the events of the tremulous Civil War era of Massachusetts's raised right arm, Cape Cod.

CHAPTER 1

ABOLITION AND POLITICS

EARLY CAPE ABOLITION ACTIVITY

Jutting forty miles off the coast of New England into the north Atlantic Ocean is the narrow, quaintly upturned Cape Cod peninsula. Some have seen in its odd shape the form of a fishhook. Others have imagined a shepherd's crook. Still others, envisioning a biceps, elbow and wrist, have called this stretch of sand the right arm of Massachusetts. Isolated and set apart, it would seem to be a refuge from the clamor of the outside world. Yet, all the disquiet of America's pre-Civil War period of 1830 to 1860—political parties restructuring, churches and church members reexamining dogma and beliefs and even feminists organizing, all because of the underlying irresolvable dilemma of slavery—found its way here. Some of the dissonance came by land and some by sea. But no matter the route, it reached this out-of-the-way land.

Some of the first serious efforts at abolishing slavery in the United States began around 1830 with the work of William Lloyd Garrison of Boston. In addition to being editor of the abolitionist newspaper *Liberator* beginning in 1831, he was instrumental in the organization of the movement and in devising the idea of putting abolitionist lecture agents into the field to touch "the depths of the people" in a grass-roots effort to instruct everyday people on the nature of slavery.[1]

Garrison's agitation for abolition collided with the forces of the status quo, embodied on the Cape by the churches and the principal newspapers, the *Barnstable Patriot* and *Yarmouth Register*. The churches supported the status quo out of fear advocacy for abolition would divide congregations. The *Patriot* and *Register* supported it because that was the position of the Democrat and Whig political parties, of which the papers were respective mouthpieces. Garrison regarded the two parties as so unprogressive and morally corrupt on the slavery question that they were best avoided in advancing his cause. Other abolitionists favored political action, possibly through a third party. Dissension over this question split American and Massachusetts abolitionism in 1839 and may explain the dissolution of the Barnstable Female Antislavery Society, which had formed a year earlier.[2]

In 1845, antislavery activity in Massachusetts had been underway around fifteen years. In that year's gubernatorial election, abolitionists fielded a candidate running under the banner of the Liberty Party. The Cape vote he received, recognizing that women did not have the ballot and that many issues besides slavery influenced voter decisions, provides a crude gauge of the local strength of the antislavery movement. The town of Eastham gave the Liberty candidate the highest percentage of Cape vote, 10 percent, followed by Sandwich and Barnstable with 9 and 8 percent respectively. At the low end were Provincetown, Truro, Wellfleet and Yarmouth that gave the Liberty standard-bearer zero votes![3]

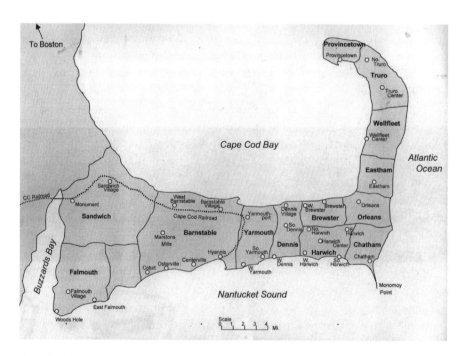

Cape Cod (Barnstable County), circa 1860. *Courtesy of the author.*

THE LECTURE CIRCUIT

The 1840s saw a great many lecturers and agents of the antislavery societies of Boston coming to the Cape in search of the souls of the people. Church activities and leaders, however, were major obstacles. Agents C.M. Burleigh and C.L. Remond reported small turnouts in 1845 in Sandwich because of a revival of "Methodism" and the minister of the Unitarian Church being "aloof" from antislavery discussions. In Harwich, they found the door of the Congregational Church bolted against their use. Better received at North Dennis, they lectured at the Unitarian Church and a schoolhouse on "the duty of the North concerning slavery," finding "the unsophisticated fishermen and sailors hung upon…every word with the interest of liberty-loving hearts."[4]

In November 1846, frequent visiting lecturer Parker Pillsbury spoke at the South Harwich Methodist Meetinghouse. Regarding the admission to the Union of Texas, Florida and Iowa as slave or free states, he discussed "the slave power of this nation [that] is now ravaging our plains…for the purpose of extending its infernal power over that region," comments underscoring the fiery nature of his oratory. His March 1847 lecture circuit began in Sandwich, continued at Centerville, Hyannis, Dennis, Brewster, Orleans and Chatham and closed at Harwich. The Centerville lecture was on a Saturday evening at the Orthodox Church. A correspondent of a third Cape newspaper, the *Sandwich Observer*, reported, "It was late before the unwearied audience was dismissed." The next day, Sunday, the Universalist Society of Osterville gave up its meeting place at "the village-house" to accommodate Pillsbury.[5]

At least one Sandwich minister, the Reverend Giles Pease of the Puritan Congregational Church, did not impede slavery discussions. He delivered an antislavery address at Centerville's Liberty Hall as part of the Fourth of July 1847 celebration. In September, William W. Brown, a former slave from Missouri, spoke at Chatham, Harwich, Hyannis, Sandwich and Falmouth, giving many Cape people their first opportunity to listen to a person who had come out of bondage. An "esteemed" woman reported that he delivered his message at Harwich so movingly that there were "few dry eyes in the audience." Sharing the platform was Pillsbury. The *Register*'s assessment of the Harwich lectures, especially those of the hard-hitting Pillsbury, is probably accurate:

> *We learn that the speeches…were of a most violent and abusive character.*
> *A[n]…abolitionist, by the name of Pillsbury, made himself peculiarly*

conspicuous by the most outrageous attacks on public men, the clergy, the government...If these men suppose that by calling hard names and indulging in low, dirty blackguardism, they are helping the cause of abolitionism, they greatly mistake the character and intelligence of our citizens.[6]

Pillsbury's 1847–1848 winter lecture circuit began at Hyannis, continued at South Dennis, Harwich, Chatham, Orleans, Brewster, Dennis, Yarmouthport and Barnstable and ended at Sandwich. Cape men donating to his cause included Alvan Howes and Ezekiel Thacher of Barnstable, and J.C. Mayo of Harwich. Meanwhile, Olive Bearse, president of the Centerville Female Antislavery Society and wife of ship captain and abolitionist Austin Bearse, held a fair at Liberty Hall, despite having "but few willing hands." She acknowledged that her crusade was a hard one. "It is much to be regretted that there is so little interest manifested among the female portion of our community, in reference to this subject." Julia Crosby Lewis assisted. Admission fee for adults was twelve and one half cents.[7]

One evening in February 1848, when Pillsbury was staying at the Bearses' house in Centerville, some women of the vicinity decided he must have some Cape Cod clam chowder. They peeled and sliced potatoes, fried pork, shelled a bucket of clams and in an hour had a soup tureen full of the best chowder he had ever had. For a few hours, the normally staid Pillsbury cut loose a little. "We had a time till midnight," he admitted in a letter to his daughter. "It was my first dissipation of the winter."[8]

FAIR IN CENTREVILLE.

The members of the Centreville Female Anti-Slavery Society anticipate holding a FAIR, on WEDNESDAY, the 16th of February next, at the Liberty Hall in this place, to be opened for public exhibition at 6 o'clock, P M., of the same day.

The object of this notice is to inform the public, and solicit aid from all who are interested in the cause for which we are laboring, which at the present time calls on us if possible more loudly than ever before to be true to our principles and to ourselves.

As it is less than a year since the formation of our Society, and we have but few willing hands, no great display can be expected; but such as we may have we present to the public, and solicit their co-operation. The smallest favors will be acceptable.

Papers friendly to the cause will please copy.
In behalf of the Society.
OLIVE BEARSE, *President.*
JULIET CROSBY, *Secretary.*
Centreville, Jan. 15, 1848.

Ad for Olive Bearse's antislavery fair in "Centreville." *Courtesy* Liberator, *February 11, 1848.*

In August 1848, an abolition rally in Harwich took place in a grove described as "about one mile south of the Congregational meetinghouse" and "near the store of Laban Snow, Jr." Featured speakers were Pillsbury, Brown, Stephen S. Foster and Lucy Stone. On the last day, Sunday, August 27, nearly 2,500 people were present; it was probably the largest Cape crowd until then to see a woman on a speaker's platform. As historian Stacey Robertson points out, female lecturers in antebellum America challenged gender norms and elicited strong reactions from audiences. Such women were called Jezebels. On this day, however, Foster, rather than Stone, drew the reaction.[9]

Speaking on the theme "Our nation's religion is a lie," Foster argued that the church in not speaking out against slavery had become the "bulwark" of it. He urged his hearers to forsake their "sin-filled" churches and "come out" from them, exhortations that tore at his audience's most innate beliefs. The setting was charged; the crowd aroused. Into this mix rushed Stillman Snow direct from his Congregational Church's service. "I'll defend the church," he shouted. "What you say is a damned lie." Violence broke out. Rioters tore up the crude plank benches and threatened to ride Foster on a rail. Women fainted. Pillsbury fled to the safety of the home of Captain Zebina H. Small, member of the rally's committee on arrangements. A somewhat roughed-up Foster escaped serious injury.[10]

CAPE COD POLITICS OF 1848

The same month as the "Harwich Mob," as the fracas was called, the Liberty or Abolitionist Party picked up the pieces of various defeats, united with dissident factions of the Democrats and Whigs in a convention at Buffalo, New York, and came away with a candidate for president in the upcoming November election—Martin Van Buren—and a new name, the Free Soilers. With the principal antislavery stance of opposition to extension of slavery into new territories and states, the new party first met on the Cape on September 2, 1848, at Barnstable Village. Attendees included Charles C. Bearse, Nathaniel Hinckley and Ansel D. Lothrop. An operative of the Democratic Party in attendance disdainfully called the Free Soilers the "loose dirt" party and confidently predicted such splinter groups would only increase the November vote for the Democrats and Whigs.[11]

The Democrats nominated Michigan senator Lewis Cass for president, and the Whigs named Mexican War hero Zachary Taylor; Millard Fillmore was his running mate. In this race, as in others of the period, the Democrats could be considered most conservative (most proslavery); the Free Soilers least most; and the Whigs most centrist. The two major parties largely avoided the slavery issue during the campaign, sticking mostly to core causes such as preservation of the Union. Two weeks before the election, *Patriot* editor and staunch Democrat Sylvanus Phinney made a remarkably prescient observation about the potential impact of the Free Soilers: "It is the most dangerous party that has ever openly taken the field. It aims at arraying the north against the south, and the south against the north, in deadly hostility which, if persisted in, will end in a dissolution of the Union."[12]

Although the Whigs and Taylor won nationally and Cape-wide, the Free Soilers polled respectably, garnering 10 percent of the national and 15 percent of the Cape vote. They did best in Sandwich, Barnstable and Harwich, where they received around 25 percent. Least supportive was Yarmouth, giving the Free Soilers just 5 percent of its vote. Almost all the rest went to the Whig general Taylor.[13]

LECTURES, MEETINGS AND FAIRS

In September 1849, Garrison himself came to the Cape. His ride from Boston to Sandwich in "the cars" was pleasurable enough, the final twenty-five miles to Harwich less so in a stage that "ploughed" through sand and enveloped him in clouds of dust. Lectures that year were at the South Harwich Methodist Meetinghouse; its use was granted by the Reverend Davis Lothrop. Assisting with arrangements were Joshua H. Robbins and Captain Gilbert Smith, both of Harwich, and Alvan Howes and Ezekiel Thacher. In November, Robbins called for the formation of Barnstable County's own antislavery society. Boston lecturer Samuel May saw great value in the new organization: "No county in New England has so much connection with the leading cities and seaports of the cotton-raising, slaveholding south as this; and no other is capable of testifying so frequently and effectively as this against the abominations of the slave system."[14] In other words, he hoped the Cape's many seamen of its extensive Southern coasting trade, witnessing slavery firsthand, would denounce it and advocate abolition.

The newly formed Barnstable County Antislavery Society met in February 1850 at the "spacious" new hall at Brewster. Its officers were Zebina H. Small and Samuel Smith of Harwich, Philander Paine of Brewster, Prince S. Crowell of East Dennis, Alvin Howes and Ezekiel Thacher. To promote the meeting, Thacher and Loring Moody of Harwich composed a jingle:

Let the sounds of traffic die—
Shut the mill-gate—leave the stall—
Fling the axe and hammer by—
Throng to Brewster Hall.[15]

That same winter, Catherine Hinckley Doane, wife of Hyannis schoolteacher Kies Doane and daughter of Hyannis resident Eli Hinckley, advertised a fair sponsored by the "females" of the Hyannis Anti-slavery Society "to be held at the old Universalist Church, Hyannis."[16]

Despite the lectures, meetings and fairs, agents found widespread indifference and opposition to abolition. An unidentified agent at Falmouth reported the town "nearly dead Anti-slavery wise." Regarding the people of Brewster, agent Daniel Foster maintained, "Moral darkness enshrouds them." At Yarmouthport, he found "the friends of humanity few and feeble there compared with Hyannis, Dennis and Harwich." Despite indifferent success, agents remained hopeful; one wrote of Falmouth "with faithful labor, it may be resuscitated and made alive."[17]

THE FUGITIVE SLAVE LAW

A provision of legislation passed by Congress in 1850 was the Fugitive Slave Law, an act mandating extradition of runaway slaves. The law led to forty-five fugitive slave prosecutions in 1851, two of them in Boston. One was Thomas Sims, who stowed away on the brig *M. and J.C. Gilmore* at Savannah and remained undiscovered until its arrival in Boston around March 6, 1851. Kimball Eldridge of Chatham was master of the *Gilmore*; Cephas I. Ames of Cotuit was the mate. Ames discovered Sims as the *Gilmore* lay in Boston harbor. Obligated by law to prevent his escape, Ames "wrung" Sims's nose, and Eldridge ran the *Gilmore* farther out into Boston harbor and had Sims locked up in the hold. He escaped, however, only to be captured on the streets of Boston.[18]

Sims underwent trial and was ordered back to his master. Because the Boston Committee of Vigilance, formed to stop slave extraditions, threatened to seize Sims, a force of two hundred men escorted him from the courthouse to the brig *Acorn*. Further discouraging seizure was two cannon and a crew "fully armed" on the *Acorn*. Henry Coombs of Barnstable was captain of the *Acorn*, and Ames was the mate. Russell Marston of Marstons Mills and Austin Bearse, both of whom moved to Boston around 1850, were members of the committee, as were Captain Enoch Lewis of Centerville and Loring Moody. Marston's "dining saloon," established in March 1851 on Mercantile Wharf, was said to be the first Boston business open to blacks.[19]

While Sims was on trial, Bearse talked with Ames and asked why he had mistreated Sims, to which Ames replied, "D—him. It was good enough for him." Bearse sadly concluded that trading with the South had turned Ames and a great many other Cape seamen into monsters. Parker Pillsbury had a similar opinion, writing that "the ship captains of Cape Cod, in their trading and coasting to the south, and transporting cotton to New England and old [England] has had a most disastrous effect on the moral feelings of these sons of the ocean."[20] The sources must be considered when weighing any possible validity of such opinions.

In another slave trial in Boston, an unknown Cape party felt that Boston politician and Osterville native Benjamin F. Hallett was too allied with Southern interests and suspended his effigy at the West Barnstable Depot. A note pinned to the effigy, dressed in a black coat, fancy pants and black hat, read, "Benj. F. Hallett, Attorney General for Southern Kidnappers. Cape Cod disowns the traitor to liberty." Attached to the coattail was a copy of the *Barnstable Patriot*, with this message: "We would have hung the editor of this paper along with him but for want of time." Hallett never saw the effigy, as it had been removed when his train stopped at West Barnstable.[21]

Symbols denoted places of abolitionist sympathy. When agent Daniel Foster traveled with Hyannis physician Thomas P. Knox over the "toilsome and expensive" twelve miles from there to Harwich in August 1852, they saw atop the cupola of a barn at a "thriving-looking place" a representation of Daniel Webster pursuing a fugitive slave woman. Inquiry at the farmhouse door revealed the owners to be Gilbert Smith and his wife, Mary Ann, who invited the travelers in.[22] In accommodating the South to preserve the Union, Webster alienated abolitionists.

THE ELECTION OF 1856

In 1854, elements of the Democrats, Whigs, old Free Soilers and various splinter parties merged and took the name Republicans. By 1856, they were organized enough to hold a national convention. An important issue of that year's presidential election was strife-ridden Kansas and whether it entered the Union as a slave or free state. The election was hotly contested between James Buchanan of the Democrats, John C. Fremont of the Republicans and Millard

Fillmore of the Whigs. Editor Phinney, supporting the conservative Buchanan–John Breckenridge ticket, wrote, "Our people need repose; they have become tired with the unceasing brawl of the Anti-Slavery, Anti-Kansas, Anti-Union brawlers." Preservation of the Union remained uppermost to the Democrats, even if it meant acquiescence to the South. A pillar of the slightly less-conservative Republicans was opposition to extension of slavery into territories.[23]

At the *Patriot* office, situated between the Custom House and a cannon on Cobb Hill east of Barnstable Village, Phinney flung out a "Buck and Breck" flag. Across the street fluttered a Fremont one between a church and a school. Editor Charles Swift of the *Register*, a Fremonter, saw symbolism in this: "Here is the true issue. The supporters of one are office and brute force, of the other religion and education. Which will you support at the ballot box?" When Republicans of Sandwich gathered on September 20, the *Patriot* dismissively reported, "The Fremont party held their *grand rally* on Saturday last...A considerable portion of the company were composed of

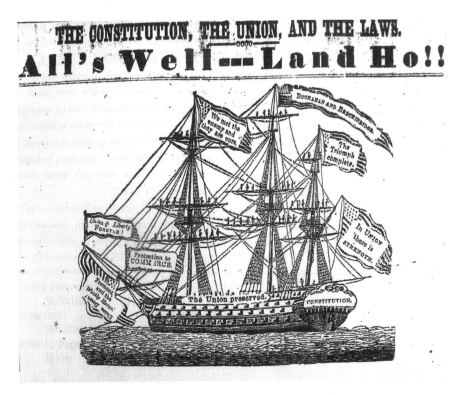

The *Barnstable Patriot* celebrates the Buchanan victory of 1856. *Courtesy* Barnstable Patriot, *November 5, 1856.*

ladies and children who were probably drawn out more by the music of the Sandwich Band than the principles of the party."[24]

Buchanan won, setting off wild celebrations among Democrats. Those of Boston fired ten thousand guns, exploded fireworks and lit barrels of tar. Special trains brought merrymakers to Barnstable Village, where the Sandwich band played and torchlight processions paraded. Provincetown's Democrats, somewhat more restrained, traveled down to James Small's hotel at Highland Light, Truro, for a supper. [25]

Beneath all the hoopla, though, was a harsh truth for the Democrats. Had it not been for Buchanan's home state of Pennsylvania and the South, the Republican Fremont would have won. The Republicans were in the ascent, at least in the North. On the Cape, they trounced the Democrats and Whigs, winning every town, with largest margins in Eastham, Orleans and Provincetown and with the smallest in Chatham. A realignment of political forces was underway.[26]

THE VIRGINIA SEARCH LAW

To prevent slaves from stowing away or being secreted aboard vessels leaving Virginia, the state instituted in March 1856 a law requiring an inspector search all departing vessels at a cost of $5.00. The following August, Captain Levi Baker of South Yarmouth, who had engaged in the Virginia coasting trade for twenty-five years, arrived at Norfolk in the schooner *Nymphas C. Hall* and loaded a cargo of corn and fruit for New Bedford. Because the fruit was liable to spoiling and an inspector unavailable, Baker cleared the state without a search. When the *Hall* returned to Norfolk a month later, under a Captain Megathlin, Virginia authorities seized the vessel.

Hearing the news, Baker went down to Norfolk where he was told he owed $700. Disinclined to hand over the money, he returned to South Yarmouth and submitted a petition, signed by one hundred of his townsmen, asking Massachusetts to test the constitutionality of the law. In preparing its case, Massachusetts officials pointed out that 120 Wellfleet oystering vessels made six trips per vessel every winter and spring to Virginia, meaning the searches cost Wellfleet $2,080 per year, $1 for every inhabitant of the town—a heavy financial burden for so small a place.

The outcome of the test case is not clear. Predictably, the *Patriot* defended the search law and compared taking slaves north out of Virginia to that state's coasting vessels stealing a horse during every visit to Massachusetts. Editor

Phinney also asked readers to consider if the $5 inspection certificate was worth "a total estrangement of feeling between the citizens of Virginia and the northern states." The *Register* opposed the search, not because it supported bringing slaves north but because dilatory inspectors arrived at their own pleasure, costing shipmasters chances to sail when fair winds sprang up.[27]

THE HYANNIS KIDNAPPING CASE

On May 1, 1859, the brig *Roleson*, with John Orlando in command, left Pensacola for Boston. A few days into the voyage, the thirty-four-year-old West Yarmouth resident discovered fugitive slave Columbus Jones on board. Orlando placed Jones in irons and tried to land him at Norfolk but could not because of unfavorable weather. On reaching Hyannis, Orlando went on shore to fetch the *Roleson*'s usual captain, Gorham Crowell, also of West Yarmouth. Meanwhile Jones broke free of his irons and started toward shore in a skiff, only to be intercepted by Crowell and Orlando as they rowed out to the *Roleson*. They returned Jones to the ship.

Learning that Hyannis mariner Edward B. Bacon was about to sail the schooner *Elizabeth B.* to Philadelphia, Crowell and Orlando paid him five hundred dollars to go out of his way and take Jones to Norfolk. When all this became known, Crowell, Orlando and Bacon were indicted and tried for kidnapping at Barnstable Superior Court. Defense attorney Caleb Cushing got an acquittal for his three defendants. "The result of this trial will be a sore and sad disappointment for the pack of howling abolitionists who have been goading it on," crowed Phinney, adding that the verdict was received with much gratification by Barnstable County's citizens. The *Boston Daily Advertiser* saw it differently, calling the trial's outcome "at variance…[with] the desires of most of the community."[28]

Around this time, Oberlin College graduates Sally Holley and Caroline Putnam spent a month lecturing on the Cape and became friends with Hyannis carpenter Francis Hinckley and his wife, Louise. Holley praised Hinckley for his condemnation of the actions of Orlando, Crowell and Bacon. She also noted that two Cape newspapers—the *Atlantic Messenger* of Hyannis, published by Edwin Coombs, and the *Provincetown Banner*—were sufficiently liberal minded to publish the writings of abolitionists. The *Banner*, outraged by the actions of the "kidnappers," declared that it was bad enough that slave catchers of the South were allowed to come into Massachusetts to catch runaways but even worse when men of Massachusetts did their work for them.[29]

END-OF-DECADE EVENTS

In a signal moment in American history, John Brown and a few followers attacked a federal arsenal at Harpers Ferry, Virginia, in October 1859 in an attempt to incite slaves to revolt against their masters. While Southerners saw in Brown's actions the potential for fulfillment of their worst dread— slave insurrections—sections of the North praised Brown and hailed him as godlike. Thus, the North–South breach widened. On the day of Brown's hanging, December 2, expressions of mourning could be heard locally. In the village of East Dennis, diarist Harriet Sears recorded that a nearby church's bells "tolled one hour." At Harwich, church bells pealed "morning, noon and evening for half an hour." Inside that place's Exchange Hall, a representation of a gallows was erected, accompanied by the inscription "John Brown—Friend of the Slave. Today Virginia gives him a martyr's grave." Thirty dollars was collected there for Brown's family.[30]

Support for Brown on the Cape was, however, far from universal. Hundreds of men, many of them leading citizens, publicly condemned him at a mass meeting at Agricultural Hall at Barnstable Village. The meeting also passed resolutions in support of the Union. Names of attendees were published in the January 3, 1860 issue of the *Patriot*.[31]

In 1859 and 1860, men of the Cape gathered signatures petitioning the Massachusetts legislature to ban Southern slave catchers from entering the state in search of runaways. Name gatherers included Henry Coombs, Alvan Howes, Russell Marston, Joshua H. Robbins, Samuel Smith, Amasa Paine of Truro and ministers Joseph R. Munsell of Harwich and William H. Stewart of South Orleans. Their work, however, was for naught because the Massachusetts Senate ruled that an "anti-man hunting law" would violate the federal Constitution.[32]

Alvan Howes, one of the Cape's more important antislavery figures, was born around 1801 in Dennis. In 1850, he placed a notice in the *Patriot* that because his wife, Mercy P. Howes, had left his "bed and board," he would no longer assume her debts. In 1854, he married fifty-three-year-old Nancy Lovell, born in Barnstable and daughter of Boston shipping agent Cornelius Lovell. According to the 1860 census, the Howeses lived east of Barnstable Village in the vicinity of Mary Dunn Road. In an uncorroborated account in the *Patriot* of April 21, 1913, Francis W. Sprague wrote that the Howeses harbored runaway slaves of the Underground Railroad at their home and that others stayed along Mary Dunn Road. Fact can be hard to separate from folklore when it comes to the Cape and the Underground Railroad, but the Howes–Mary Dunn story seems credible. Mary Dunn was a black woman who lived in the woods "about two miles from Barnstable Village."[33]

THE ELECTION OF 1860

April 13, 1860, was a glorious spring day in New England. The long winter was over; the rain from the day before had ended; and the sun was warm. The day was even more special at Boston's Central Wharf. Standing at their posts on the Merchants and Miners Steamship Line's *S.R. Spaulding*, Captain Solomon Howes and Mate Joshua Atkins Jr. of Chatham, but living in Boston, made ready to cast loose with their New England delegation for the Democratic national convention at Charleston. From alongside watched former Hyannis residents George H. Hallett and Danforth F.W. Parker, officers of the *Spaulding*'s sister steamer, *William Jenkins*. Bunting adorned both vessels. At 5:00 p.m., the hour of sailing, the activity climaxed. Crowds on the wharf cheered and a twenty-piece brass band on board played as starboard and port field pieces discharged, the valves of the ship lifted and the *Spaulding* departed.

Unfortunately for the Democrats, this was the high point of the trip. The convention at Charleston deadlocked over slavery and adjourned without a presidential nominee. At Chicago, the Republicans nominated Abraham Lincoln. Knowing little about him and caring less, Phinney wondered what Mr. Lincoln knew besides splitting rails. When Phinney called him "an illiterate western boor," Swift of the *Register* countered that Lincoln's education didn't matter so much, that more importantly he was a man of the people.[34]

Despite a large September rally at Barnstable Village in which a thirty-foot-long banner for Democratic presidential nominee John Breckenridge was carried through the streets, the Democrats were swimming against the tide. Lincoln activist groups called "Wide-awakes," who wore uniforms of black-glazed caps with a red band and black-glazed capes, sprang up. Dennis had a chapter, as did Sandwich. Forty Sandwich Wide-awakes marched on October 3, 1860, at a huge rally at Wareham.[35]

Lincoln carried the election by winning almost all the states north of the Potomac and Ohio Rivers. On the Cape, he crushed Breckenridge and two other candidates, taking over 70 percent of the vote. The Democrats, conservatives as usual in the election, did best in Falmouth, Barnstable and Chatham. Phinney called Lincoln's victory one of sectionalism over nationalism. Rodney Baxter of Hyannis, captain of the Boston and Southern Steamship Line's *South Carolina*, was in Charleston when the people there heard of Lincoln's election. On bringing his steamer into Boston, he reported South Carolina resolved to leave the Union.[36]

Thus was the state of political and moral affairs with the thirty-six thousand people of Cape Cod at the eve of they knew not what. With the rest of the North, they had voted against extension of slavery and perceived pro-Southern policies of President Buchanan, for paid over slave labor. The cause, however, uppermost to Cape voters in the election was preservation of the Union. This they demonstrated by subjugating economic self-interest—the Southern coast trade—to support, overwhelmingly, the Illinois backwoodsman deemed most trustworthy not to abandon the Union, whatever the cost. In many ways, the election of Lincoln was, for the people of the Cape, the culmination of a long road on the slavery question and its accompanying politics. They, like Lincoln and the nation, stood at the precipice.[37]

CHAPTER 2

FIRST BLOOD

Apprehension and Uncertainty

Rodney Baxter's report was accurate. South Carolina, resolved to leave the Union over the election of Abraham Lincoln, did just that. On December 20, 1860, the legislature of the Palmetto State enacted an ordinance of secession, shrinking the Union from thirty-four to thirty-three states. "The times are such as have not transpired from the days of Washington until now," wrote *Patriot* editor Phinney for his New Year's Day 1861 issue. One of the first Cape Codders to witness the changed times was Kimball Ryder of Chatham. When he left Charleston for Boston in the bark *Modena* in January 1861, it was as if he were leaving a foreign country. On his clearance papers, port officials had crossed out the words "United States of America" and replaced them with "Sovereign and Independent State of South Carolina."[1]

Fearing seizure of Forts Taylor and Jefferson at or near Key West, Florida, the War Department chartered the Merchants and Miners steamer *Joseph Whitney*, with Winslow Loveland of Chatham commanding, for a mission to reinforce them. On board for her January 10, 1861 departure from Boston were a detachment of soldiers and artillerymen. After the artillerymen determined Fort Jefferson needed more firepower, Loveland took his steamer to Key West where they procured guns and brought them to the fort. The *Whitney*'s timely mission helped keep Key West in the Union. Over time it became a vital logistical base for Union military operations in Florida, the West Indies and Gulf of Mexico.[2]

After Texas seceded on February 1, 1861, U.S. troops stationed at El Paso's Fort Bliss and other posts around the state got the distinct feeling they were no longer welcome. Fearing attack from a hostile population, their commanding officer requested evacuation of his 1,330 officers and men. Accordingly, the War Department chartered the *Empire City* and her running mate *Star of the West* of a New York–New Orleans steamship line, captained respectively by Barnstable men Samuel S. Baxter and Elisha Howes. Both vessels left New York on March 12 for the Texas coast.

The *Empire City* on April 13 took aboard her complement of evacuees near Indianola, Texas, and left for New York. However, those slated for the *Star of the West* had to camp twenty miles away since there was no closer fresh water supply. While Howes awaited their arrival, Confederate forces pretending to be the anticipated U.S. troops steamed alongside his steamer, came aboard and captured her. When ordered to surrender, Howes exclaimed, "The hell you say! I suppose I have no choice as your men far outnumber mine, but I call this a damned scurvy trick." He and his crew went to New Orleans as captives on their steamer, which was then a prize to the Confederacy. From there, they made their way "by a circuitous route" to New York, where Howes filed an official protest.[3]

Ad for steamer *Star of the West. Courtesy* Boston Daily Courier, *September 8, 1859.*

In the uneasy and uncertain winter and spring of 1861, as North and South groped along neither at war nor peace, commerce between the two sections continued. Cyrus Nickerson of Dennis took the schooner *E. Nickerson* on her usual run to City Point and Richmond, Virginia, while the ship *Vitula*, captained by Ira Bursley of Barnstable, loaded at Liverpool for Mobile. An upstart Onan Bacon flew the Stars and Stripes as his coasting schooner *W.R. Newcomb* received corn at Fredericksburg, Virginia.[4]

When reconciliation hopes glimmered in midwinter, suspended steamship service between Boston and Charleston resumed February 22, with Rodney Baxter steering the *South Carolina* for Charleston. The service was short-lived, however. After leaving Boston on April 6, stress of weather forced him to take his vessel into Norfolk. Learning there of a highly agitated state of affairs in South Carolina, he landed his passengers and returned north, arriving in Boston unexpectedly.[5]

War!

The only spark needed to ignite the North–South tinderbox was an incident. On April 12, South Carolinians fired on Fort Sumter. In an aroused and indignant North, Lincoln called for seventy-five thousand volunteer militia to serve three months to put down the rebellion. The response was rapid, especially in Massachusetts, where there had been a long tradition of building up and maintaining militia units. In 1859, the entire Bay State militia of over five thousand men had encamped at Concord, an event unprecedented for peacetime America. Because of this high state of readiness, four regiments of Massachusetts soldiers went off to war on April 18, just three days after Massachusetts senator Henry Wilson wired Governor John Andrew to send them.[6]

Amid "unbounded applause" at Boston's Central Wharf on April 18, one of the four regiments, the Third, went aboard the *S.R. Spaulding*. Forty-eight hours later, the regiment went ashore at Fortress Monroe, Virginia. From there, the *Spaulding* proceeded to Baltimore to take on a return cargo. However, as she approached the city, a tug came out to warn that two hundred Southern sympathizers planned to seize the steamer on her arrival. On hearing this, Captain Howes turned his steamer seaward, foiling the plot. Another of the four regiments, the Fourth, left Fall River for Fortress Monroe on the steamer *State of Maine*, with Oliver Eldridge of Yarmouth commanding. As he was leaving Virginia, authorities tried to implement

An 1861 view of Fortress Monroe, Virginia. *Courtesy U.S. Army Heritage and Education Center.*

the search law and examine his ship for secreted slaves. A defiant Eldridge rebuffed the authorities, telling them they were now dealing with the laws of the United States. "You have been preaching all your lives," he barked, "that Yankees are a pack of misers and cowards, and won't fight. Now you'll have…opportunity to test the accuracy of your opinion on that point."[7]

Soldiers on the *Spaulding* included Sandwich's George H. Freeman and Monument's Howard Burgess, Charles M. Packard and brothers Sylvester O. and William W. Phinney. Woods Hole's George W. Washburn was on the *State of Maine*. These six thus became the first Cape soldiers to go off to war and set foot on seceded soil. The prompt arrival of Massachusetts troops at Fortress Monroe helped prevent its seizure by the Confederates. Like the Key West forts, it proved immensely valuable. Also going to the front early were Wellfleet natives Hawes Atwood Jr. and Joseph W. Paine and Orleans native Elkanah Crosby, members of the Somerville Guards of the Fifth Regiment, which reached Washington ten days after the war began.[8]

BARNSTABLE COUNTY AWAKE!

With the start of hostilities, Cape towns resounded with meetings and rallies. The first was on Saturday evening, April 19, at Sandwich Town Hall. After speeches and "spirit-stirring" music by the town brass band, it was announced that the town would offer a company of around 50 three-months' soldiers to the governor. During Provincetown's meeting on April 22, dentist Albion S. Dudley presented a revolver to Rawlins T. Atkins and urged him to use it "efficiently." He and Paron C. Paine were the town's first volunteers. Captain Stephen A. Ryder and others hoisted the national flag on High Hill. Yarmouth citizens met the same day at Village Hall, where the presence of "ladies" graced the large audience. A day later, an assemblage of Brewster townspeople cheered as the Stars and Stripes went aloft at Schoolhouse Number Two. A rally at North Sandwich on May 1 closed with a supper at the house of Captain Seth Briggs.[9]

Also aroused was Falmouth. A salute of guns followed a flag-raising on May 8 at the academy and schoolhouse. A day later, a citizens gathering at Town Hall discussed formation of a coast guard and sang "America." On May 11, the packet *Bride* brought from New Bedford a big gun, purchased by townsmen. Up Buzzards Bay at a Pocasset rally, red, white and blue adorned the heads of ladies, stars and stripes the aprons of girls and union badges the lapels of gentlemen. Truro citizens erected three liberty poles. The largest, crafted by Provincetown ships carpenter/spar maker Isaac Collins, was on a hill north of Wilder's Store in Truro Center. At West Harwich, five hundred people cheered and the Harwich brass band entertained as a flag was lifted to the breeze.[10]

The Sandwich company offered to the governor had its beginnings as a militia unit known as the Sandwich Guards, formed around June of 1860. The motivation for its formation may have been the publicity generated by the Concord encampment of the previous fall. Charles Chipman became captain of the company, which marched in Cape parades in the summer of 1860.[11]

When the company arrived in Boston on May 6, 1861, to sail to Fortress Monroe, its men learned they had new orders to serve not three months but three years! Since they were unprepared for so long an absence, they returned on May 10 to Sandwich. After some thought, almost all agreed to the change. For the next week, the town was a beehive. Town tailors volunteered to cut soldiers' uniforms while ladies sewed them. All was ready May 18. In morning ceremonies at Town Hall, editor Phinney of the *Patriot* presented the unit a blue banner, with one side bearing the figure of a raised arm grasping the sword of liberty with words above reading "The Right Arm of Old Massachusetts." Shortly afterward, escorted by the cornet band, the men marched to the waiting "cars," traveled to Boston, received a supper given by the agent of the Boston and Sandwich Glassworks and, at the end of a busy day, embarked on the steamer *Cambridge*—with Seleck H. Matthews of Yarmouth as captain—for Fortress Monroe. It was the first Cape military unit to go to the front.[12]

Fourth of July 1861 festivities on the Cape had a martial flavor. With its fishing fleet at home, Wellfleet celebrated exuberantly. After a parade from the Congregational to the Methodist Church led by the Provincetown Band, celebrators dined beneath a spacious tent, while the band and a glee club provided music "chiefly of a national character." Also enjoying dinner in a tent were six hundred people of Harwichport. Afterward, Watson B. Kelley and a choir sang "the popular air of 'New Dixie,'" a tune the crowd liked so much it called for it again. Chatham citizens fired guns at sunrise, while at Marstons Mills, the Zouaves of West Barnstable and a rifle company of the Plains marched to Benjamin Marston's residence on Freedom Hill for "appropriate exercises." At Falmouth, the Horribles carrying a Succonesset Guards banner paraded through the village.[13]

CONCERNS AND CAPTURES

Within days of the start of the war, President Jefferson Davis of the Confederacy called on private citizens to arm vessels and attack Union high seas commerce. In response, on May 13, a large number of Boston shipping agents and marine insurers petitioned Secretary of the Navy Gideon Welles to station an armed steamer as a "Coast Guard" in Vineyard Sound. They justified this request by pointing out that the number of vessels passing through the sound was "very large, amounting to more than fifty thousand annually, and belonging to all the ports of New England." Several sound-facing Cape towns took action. Harwich citizens called for a "well-armed" steamer to patrol between Monomoy Point and the mouth of Vineyard Sound, while Chatham passed resolutions in favor of a coast guard. Ezra Crowell headed a Home and Coast Guard organized at Falmouth.[14]

The navy's resources were too thin in the spring of 1861 to protect Vineyard Sound or other seaways. Shipmasters ventured out at their peril. When Joshua Myrick of West Dennis left New York for Norfolk in mid-April in the schooner *Sprightling Sea*, Virginia was still in the Union. When he arrived April 20, it had just seceded and become the enemy—poor timing for sure. The Virginians seized his schooner, bored holes in her bottom, sunk her in the ship channel and pressed part of the crew into Confederate service. Myrick—who collected nothing for his freight—escaped by hiding in a wrecking schooner and then taking another schooner to New York. He left Dixie with but twenty-five cents in his pocket, owning the dubious honor of first Cape ship and captain captured of the Civil War.[15]

Also unprotected was Yarmouth shipmaster George Loring, who was loading hard pine lumber in Georgia's Satilla River. After starting his brig *Elisha Doane* for the north on May 3, a Confederate privateer overhauled it and held him and his crew captive; eight days later, it released them and allowed them to continue. Engaged in cutting cedar and live oak for the navy in the South were 1852 Harvard graduate Elijah Swift and two other Falmouth men, Leonard Doty and James N. Parker. The three barely eluded capture. Swift had cut and prepared for market thirty-thousand cubic feet of live oak ship timber during the winter of 1859–1860 at Mosquito Inlet, Florida. Still unshipped when the war came, Swift and his father Oliver wrote the Navy Department about it.[16]

Besides Joshua Myrick, another West Dennis schooner master felt the impact of the war's outbreak. Orrin Lewis had habitually sailed the *Satilla* between Annapolis and Norfolk, but on April 29, the navy notified him to forego entering Norfolk and head instead for a port north of Cape Henlopen, Delaware. Also feeling the impact was Barnstable ship co-owner John T. Hall. His *Abaellino* left Boston for New Orleans on April 4 with a cargo of ice worth $20,000. On May 18, the Confederate privateer *Ivy* captured the *Abaellino* in the Mississippi River. In 1863, the *Abaellino*'s owners sued for nonpayment of the freight but the defense countered that the plaintiffs knew the risks of imminent war and dispatched their ship and cargo anyway.[17]

Whalers at sea had little way of knowing war had begun. When the privateer *Calhoun* on May 24 approached the schooner *Mermaid* seventy miles south of New Orleans and ordered her to heave to, Captain Robert Soper of Provincetown, "entirely ignorant of the political state of the country," didn't understand he was being taken as a prize. The privateer towed the *Mermaid*—plus Provincetown whaling vessels *Panama* and *John Adams*—into New Orleans. Although left without money "to shift for themselves," Soper and several of his comrades left the city by rail on June 3, traveled unbothered through Tennessee and Kentucky and reached Boston on June 8. Two days after the whaler captures, the Union navy established a blockade of the Mississippi River's outlets below New Orleans (or "passes" as they were called), stopping privateering there.[18]

Because so many ships were being seized, Galveston shipping agents—even ardently secessionist ones—became concerned in June that their commerce would be compromised. Learning this, military leaders ordered the agents *not* to communicate with and warn approaching ships about risk of capture. Thus, when Yarmouth/Barnstable captain Joshua H. Eldridge arrived on June 3, sixty-five days from Liverpool with his sick wife, Susan, aboard, he was not warned, and his bark *Nueces* was seized. Agent Ebenezer Nichols felt so bad about this he opened his plantation to Eldridge and secured him passage north through Confederate lines, enabling him to reach Boston on June 15. Five weeks later, his wife died.[19]

Despite the Mississippi River blockade, the Confederate commerce raider *Sumter* on June 29 slipped into the Gulf of Mexico. Once there, it pounced on Union merchant ships, one of them the schooner *Abby Bradford*. The *Abby B.*, built 1860, named for the young daughter of Captain Ezra Freeman of Sandwich and adorned with a full statue of a little girl as the figurehead, was captured on July 25 off the coast of Venezuela. Gaining a touch of redemption for letting the *Sumter* slip out, the Union navy recaptured the *Abby B.* on August 13 while a Confederate prize crew was taking her into the Mississippi River. She went to prize court in Philadelphia, was restored to her owner and, in October, was back in Freeman's command.[20]

Although the Union navy was strong enough in the summer of 1861 to stop privateering at the passes, it was not strong enough to stop it in North Carolina. Simeon Backus left Cuba on June 20 in the schooner *Herbert Manton* with 245 hogsheads of molasses and sugar and proceeded north in the Gulf Stream. His course put him off Hatteras on July 3, just as privateer activity there intensified. The privateer *Winslow* captured the *Manton* and took her, Backus and crew to New Bern. After imprisonment, the men were put aboard Halifax, Nova Scotia–bound vessels on July 23. Backus finally reached his home in Osterville on August 16.[21]

As for the *Manton*, the Confederates at New Bern unloaded her valuable $30,000 cargo and sank her in the river to obstruct shipping traffic. After Union forces captured the town in March 1862, she was raised, refloated and brought alongside the wharf. Union naval officer Luke Chase of Hyannisport, stationed at New Bern, assisted with the *Manton*'s refitting and, on June 4, he wrote that he was hopeful she could be gotten "to America by the 3rd of July, one year from the time she was stolen." He did even better. On June 24, she was back in Centerville with owner Lewis Crosby. Later that year, she was chartered as a government transport, with Ephraim Crowell commanding. Furthermore, when the Confederate raider *Tacony* menaced New England in 1863, the navy armed the *Manton*, put a naval captain and crew aboard and sent her on a two-week search cruise. The end for this remarkable schooner came around 1880 when she had to be abandoned at sea.[22]

If an observation of the crew of the steamer *Potomska* can be believed, a privateer even got into Cape waters. On July 14, 1861, the steamer's men reported that "a brig was seen from our wheelhouse, off Cape Cod, chasing a schooner. After a while the brig was seen to fire…We suppose it was the Jeff Davis." Joseph W. Nye of Falmouth was *Potomska*'s captain, and Ward Eldridge of Woods Hole was the mate. At Hatteras on July 25, the North Carolina privateer *Mariner* captured the schooner *Nathaniel Chase*, with Daniel Doane of Harwichport captain. The captors put crewman William T. Phillips of Harwich to work on a schooner plying between Hatteras and New Bern. Later, faced with forced enlistment in the Confederate army or working in a soldier's mess, he chose the latter. After a month of such work, he escaped and made his way to the *S.R. Spaulding*, by which he reached New York. The Confederates sank the *N. Chase* at Newbern whereupon Union forces, like the *Manton*, refloated her and returned her to her owners.[23]

War ended the Boston and Southern Steamship Line's service to Charleston and with it Rodney Baxter's position of captain of its *South Carolina*. The Union navy, however, came to the rescue, purchasing and commissioning her as well as her running mate, the *Massachusetts*. The navy also gave Baxter his old job back, in a sense. He received an appointment as a navy officer and orders to the USS *South Carolina*. He was, however, no longer captain but a ship's officer, a position he may have found awkward. Serving under him was his half-brother Horatio N. Baxter.

After the *South Carolina* blockaded Galveston in early July 1861, it captured the schooner *George G. Baker*, and Horatio Baxter and five other *South Carolina* crewmen headed north with the prize. Off Hatteras on August 8, the little privateer *York*, mounting but one gun, captured the *Baker*, put Baxter and party on the *York*, placed a Confederate prize crew on the *Baker* and headed for Hatteras. Just off the light, a Union blockader began pursuing the pair. The crew of the *York* ran their vessel ashore, set it afire and escaped, taking Baxter and party with them. Captured for a third time, the *Baker* finally got to New York, under a second Union prize crew. Baxter spent time as a prisoner of war.[24]

A casualty on land was Yarmouth-native Philander Crowell Jr. His unit, Company G of the First Massachusetts Regiment, bore much of the July 18, 1861 attack by Confederate forces at Blackburn's Ford, Virginia. After receiving a slight wound, a comrade took Crowell on his back to remove him from the field. While being carried, however, a bullet struck him in the head, making him the first Cape-connected death in action of the war. His brother Arthur, in Washington at the time, came to the battlefield, retrieved the body and took it to the family home at Chelsea, where the deceased received a hero's funeral. Unhurt at Blackburn's Ford were Rawlins T. Atkins and Paron Paine, also of the Massachusetts First. Three days later, Marstons

Mills's Enoch Crocker died in the Battle of Bull Run, and Falmouth's John B. Landers was wounded. Keeping Washington updated on the battle was former Truro telegraph operator William C. Hall, now in a vital Union army arm in the United States Military Telegraph Corps. Around this time, the Confederates captured Telegraph Corpsman I.S. Duruin, former operator at Yarmouthport, and pressed him into similar service on their side.[25]

END OF THE WARM-UP

As August 1861 ended, hostilities had been underway five months. The Cape had put its first body of soldiers in the field and others of its men in scattered Massachusetts and Northern state regiments. Southern privateers had had their day and more powerful vessels—the commerce raiders—were about to supersede them. In the largest battle to date, the South had badly beaten the North at Bull Run. The Cape's vital coasting economy was in the doldrums because of the loss of Southern ports and fear of privateers. The Cape people may or may not have been mindful of it, but they were up against a formidable foe. They no longer were putting down a rebellion. Rather, they were in a war—one that would require a long struggle to carry to its finish.

CHAPTER 3

CAPE COD AND THE NAVY

A National Force

One result of President Jefferson Davis's call for his fellow Southerners to arm vessels and attack Union marine commerce was the stirring of Boston shipping merchant Robert B. Forbes into motion. On April 17, 1861, he called on the merchants and seamen of Massachusetts to organize, outfit and prepare for action a state coast guard corps. A day later Governor Andrew acknowledged Forbes's idea, calling it "a proposition which the piratical manifesto of Mr. [Jefferson] Davis...fully justifies." Andrew tempered his response, however, pointing out that Massachusetts law prevented financial support of such an entity.[1]

Undeterred, Forbes pressed his idea forward. Israel Lombard of Truro and David Snow of Orleans pledged five hundred dollars each. George Marston of Barnstable reported Cape Cod as supportive. In late June and early July 1861, Commodore Forbes took his coast guard of eighty men dressed in navy blue uniforms and equipped with banner, side arms, four launches and one brass howitzer per launch on an excursion around the state, relying on the "hospitality" of the towns for their subsistence. They reached Provincetown on July 5, marched through town, fired their howitzers and put on a good show. From there, they crossed Cape Cod Bay to Barnstable Village, arriving at low tide. Waist deep in mud and eel grass, they tugged their howitzers ashore where the men—some having lost their breeches in the ooze—boarded the "cars" and proceeded to Hyannis for a "sumptuous" supper and "splendid" ball.[2]

Forbes wanted the Navy Department to accept his state coast guard for national naval service, just as the War Department was doing with

Massachusetts-raised army units. Navy Secretary Welles, however, wanting a national naval force under one command, refused Forbes's request, characterizing his coast guard as "a voluntary, patriotic association not subject to the laws...of the Navy" and "more than questionable." He did not want to follow the War Department's practice of accepting state volunteer units, which came complete with their own officers. Unable to sway Welles, Forbes sold his launches and disbanded his coast guard.[3]

The idea of state-based naval units did not vanish. When privateers escaped the Union naval blockade of the Southern coastline in mid-July, moved into New England waters and put Massachusetts marine interests on edge, Governor Andrew himself wrote Welles. Arguing that "the most stringent measures are not [being] adopted to strengthen the blockade and scour every privateer from our seas," he requested authority to send out a fleet of armed New England coasters as a "naval corps of volunteers." Welles again refused, for the same reason as in the Forbes request. To fend off propositions such as Forbes and Andrew's for "yacht squadrons...naval brigades" and other "schemes of private adventure" (which tended toward Northern privateering), and additionally to destroy Southern privateering and create an "effective" blockade, Welles and Congress framed and passed the "Act to Provide for the Temporary Increase of the Navy," approved on July 25, 1861.[4]

The navy legislation opened the way for merchant ship captains and mates to receive officer berths in the Union navy. All these men needed for a position were favorable letters of recommendation from persons under or with whom they had sailed, passed examinations and signed oaths of allegiance. Their appointments were effective for the duration of the insurrection.[5] From the Cape came some 170 of these "emergency" officers.

Besides providing for additional officers, the legislation authorized Secretary Welles to purchase vessels. One of his first was the bark *Dawn*, which Luke Chase had sailed for four years as a hides-and-wool vessel between Buenos Aires and New York. Both the *Dawn* and Chase received commissioning in the fall of 1861; *Dawn* as renamed navy ship *Midnight*, and Chase as a navy officer, as both entered new lines of work. Another purchase was the bark *Gemsbok*, with Simeon Mayo of Orleans the captain. Also a hides ship, she had regular service between Boston and Cape Town, South Africa, after launching in 1857. Upon reaching Boston on July 11, 1861, navy agents bought the bark. Commissioned USS *Gemsbok* on August 30th, she made a capture three weeks later.[6]

The notion of state naval units reappeared in 1862. Early that year, navy agents from Boston scoured the Cape for two hundred seamen, mostly to serve in Commodore David Porter's mortar schooner fleet in an expedition to the lower Mississippi River. An anonymous correspondent of the *Patriot* doubted the navy would get the men, gave the reason he felt that way and suggested a way to attract them. "No man," he wrote, "can know when he enlists [in the navy] who is to be his commander…I will venture to say there would be no trouble to officer and man a Gun Boat from every town on the Cape, if they would select the commander from each town, as there are competent men that have had sufficient experience already… to take command."[7]

The anonymous correspondent's doubt was on target. Even though the navy's campaign included authorizing Dr. George Shove of Yarmouth to do the fitness examinations for men for the mortar flotilla, few volunteered. Only one recruit, George White of Harwich, can be verified. It may indeed be that Cape seamen were concerned about service under a commanding officer who was a stranger. On this point, the army had a distinct advantage. When Godfrey Rider Jr. of Provincetown advertised for army volunteers in the summer of 1862, his sales pitch had a down-home ring: "He is a man who has always lived on Cape Cod and one who

Ad soliciting Cape seamen in early 1862. *Courtesy* Barnstable Patriot, *January 14, 1862.*

thoroughly understands the needs of Cape men." The navy couldn't match that sort of language.[8]

Further damaging navy recruiting was the matter of the sailors of the steamer *Massachusetts*. When that vessel completed its blockading cruise of 1861–1862 and returned in February to New York, its men's enlistments had expired and they rightfully expected to be paid. However, a month later, they had received nothing. With expenses of staying at the Sailors Home mounting, they entreated Senator Henry Wilson to look into their situation. The men, described by the home's superintendent as "unusually sober and steady," hailed mostly from Taunton. One, however, George H. Backus, was from Hyannis.[9]

CATCHING THE FISHERMEN

Many years before the Civil War, Congress enacted a fishing bounty. Its purpose was two-fold: assist cod fishermen with the cost of salt, on which duties were steep, and induce young men to become sailors and thus insure the navy a supply of ordinary seamen in an emergency, such as war with England. Though these reasons had lost their relevance in the 1850s, the bounty remained. To the South, it was anathema—a protectionist measure partial to one section of the country and another seed for discord.

The Cape newspaper editors contended that the fishermen, having accepted the bounty, should reciprocate and give back service as sailors to the navy in this, its hour of need. There was just one problem: the fishermen weren't biting at the idea. "Where are the sailors?" asked the perplexed editor of the *Register*. Phinney of the *Patriot* warned the fishermen that their bounty was in "great peril" for not offering themselves for the mortar flotilla. What the newspapermen weren't taking into account was that fishermen could receive another bounty—for army enlistment. In contrast, the navy had no enlistment bounty, which was another recruiting disadvantage. Also, since army enlistments counted against town recruiting quotas and navy ones didn't, recruitment rallies on the Cape and around the state emphasized army enlisting.[10]

Beyond the enlistment bounty, fishermen chose the army because they didn't have to pay for their clothes, and they earned approximately one hundred dollars more per year than in the navy. Bad timing also victimized navy recruiting of fishermen on the Cape. When the *Gemsbok* ran short of crewmen in the summer of 1862, assistant navy secretary Fox sent it to

Provincetown to recruit fishermen. At first, Captain Edward Cavendy was optimistic about his prospects. Realizing, however, a few days later that the fishermen were still out with their fleets, he wrote that his prospects were poor. Even the imposing navy frigate *Sabine* failed to make an impact. Sent to Provincetown to replenish crew in the fall of 1863 *after* the fishermen had returned, she failed to get even a nibble.[11]

Issues of pay, unease about serving under an unknown commanding officer and misunderstandings about fishing and fishermen doomed the navy to poor recruitment results on the Cape the first few years of the war. Any doubt of this is removed by simply looking over the roster of Cape volunteers enlisting in the army for that period and seeing the large number who listed their occupation as seamen. One final handicap under which the navy labored was the draft rules. Amazingly, men who had done a navy enlistment went on to the draft list. This inequity and the one in quotas were corrected in 1864.[12]

PILOTS

To thread its ships up narrow tidal rivers, to finesse them across shallows bars, to guide them through obstruction-laden backwaters, the navy relied on pilots. These were men competent enough with charts to be entrusted to the steering of navy vessels. Lives and valuable government property rested on their skills. Unfortunately, records relating to pilots are fragmentary. Because of this, the discussion given here is necessarily incomplete. Undoubtedly there were others from the Cape besides these nineteen.

Pilots were of two types, uniformed and nonuniformed. Uniformed ones were navy officers who had passed a pilot's examination entitling them to an additional one hundred dollars per month. The Cape's only such pilots were John W. Godfrey and William Haffords. Nonuniformed ones, having no navy appointment, were not entitled to furloughs. Also, Cape towns received no credit for them in enlistment quotas. Ebenezer Crowell of West Yarmouth, a nonuniformed pilot on the *South Carolina* during the first few months of the war, brought a prize to New York around August 1861. Bradford S. Norris of Hyannis and Thaddeus Brown of South Yarmouth piloted on the army transport *Empire City* and naval steamer *R.B. Forbes* at the capture of Port Royal, South Carolina, in November 1861. Haffords was also there as a pilot. In early 1862, D.F.W. Parker was pilot of the large troop ship *Mississippi*. In the advance of the ironclads on Fort Sumter, South

Carolina, on April 7, 1863, William Evans of Dennis and Davis Crowell of West Yarmouth piloted on the flagship *Ben Deford* while Haffords and Godfrey piloted other vessels. George W. Bacon of Hyannis was pilot on the steamer *DeMolay* when it transported the first black regiment recruited in the North, the famous Fifty-fourth Massachusetts, from Boston to South Carolina in May 1863.[13]

Piloting could be hazardous. In 1863, John W. Small of Provincetown was pilot on the navy steamer *Mount Washington*. When Confederate forces attacked along the Nansemond River of Virginia, his and other vessels went to the assistance of the army. On April 14, his vessel took heavy fire; Small was severely wounded, and he died a month later. Other Provincetown pilots were Lemuel Cook and Paul Dyer. Fifty-eight-year-old Cook, recommended by Robert B. Forbes, served on the steamer *Wyandotte* from March 1863 to March 1864. Dyer was on the steamer *Western World*. Others who piloted were Josiah C. Parker of Hyannis (a brother-in-law of both Norris and William A. Hallett, captain of the *Deford*), Joshua Hallett of Hyannis, Joseph Baxter of Dennis, Thomas C. Hardy of Chatham, Ephraim Lewis of Centerville, John Bodfish of Barnstable and Luther Handy of Pocasset.[14]

THE *MONITOR* AND THE *MERRIMAC*

On March 8, 1862, the Confederate ironclad *Merrimac* steamed out into Hampton Roads, Virginia, and rammed the wooden Union naval frigate *Cumberland*, killing many men, among them Josiah Freeman of Provincetown and Holmes Nickerson of Wellfleet. Arriving too late that day to save the *Cumberland* was the Union ironclad *Monitor*. The next day, in one of the great events of the nineteenth century, she dueled with the *Merrimac*. Aboard the *Monitor* as pilot was Frederick Nickerson of South Dennis.[15]

Arriving at Hampton Roads around the same time as the *Monitor* was none other than Phinney of the *Patriot*, who had come down from Baltimore on a government steamer. As the sun rose on March 9, he watched the unfolding action from his ship. He was not alone. Hundreds of spectators gazed from decks and rigging of other vessels and from shore as the little *Monitor*, untested in battle and armed with just two guns, went up against the ponderous and battle-proven *Merrimac*, described as resembling a submerged house with just the roof showing. Acquitting herself well in the duel, the *Monitor* was an object of praise for Phinney, who concluded that the event he had so fortuitously been able to witness would "revolutionize all naval warfare."[16]

Like two prizefighters sitting in their corners, the two iron ships awaited the moment to renew their bout. Into this setting arrived the brig *Sabao*, with David H. Baker of West Dennis as captain and co-owner and neighbor Simeon Crowell as crewman. On board were 250 bales of hay, loaded at Portsmouth, New Hampshire, under government charter for delivery to the Chesapeake Bay area. As the brig awaited orders off Hampton Bar the night of April 12, the *Merrimac*'s cohort *Jamestown* captured and burned her. Crowell and other crewmen were taken to the Confederate States Military Prison. When Baker asked why he'd not received protection from navy gunboats, authorities at Fortress Monroe replied that such a response might draw the *Merrimac* out prematurely, as they were hoping to decoy it out at a moment of their choosing to destroy it. Since Baker never delivered his hay, the government denied his claim for damages.[17]

MARINES

The Marine Corps, allied with the navy, was a small, rather insignificant branch of service during the Civil War. In the fall of 1861, Colonel William A. Howard formed the New York Marine Artillery, a unit designed for amphibious duty. Luke B. Chase recruited for Colonel Howard before he received his navy officer appointment. Other Cape men who served under Howard were Captain Charles G. Baker and Lieutenant Benjamin D. Baxter of Hyannis, Lloyd B. Hamblin of Barnstable, William E. Tupper and William H. Chipman of Provincetown and Hawes Atwood, who enlisted after his ninety-day army enlistment expired.[18]

Colonel Howard's marines were part of General Ambrose Burnside's expedition in early 1862 to seize control of North Carolina's inland waterways. Captain Baker, in command of the army gunboat *Pioneer*, was in the "hottest of the fire" in the capture of Roanoke Island, the expedition's chief objective. Baxter was on the army gunboat *Vidette*. Acting more like sailors than marines, he and his men bombarded enemy shore positions and covered troop landings. Shells from his gun exploded on the beach of the island with enough force to send jets of sand twenty feet into the air. In July, marine Tupper, "much beloved by all who knew him," died of illness in New Bern, North Carolina.[19]

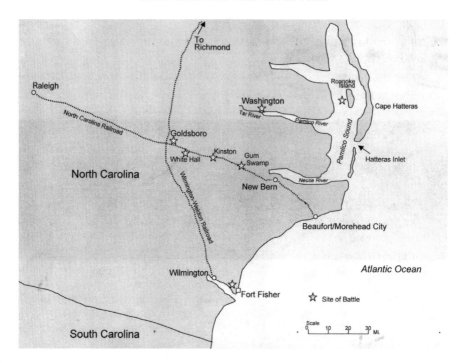

Civil War North Carolina. *Courtesy of the author.*

CLOSING THE LOG

Despite Massachusetts's ups and downs with the navy over the course of the war, it nonetheless massively supported that branch of service, furnishing nearly twenty thousand men, or about 1.4 percent of the state's total population. Only New York furnished more.[20] And who knows? Perhaps sprinkled through those twenty thousand might have even been a few of those elusive Cape Cod fishermen!

CHAPTER 4

THE TRANSPORTS

INTRODUCTION

Cape Cod's vital coasting schooner industry, in an economic downturn in 1861, rebounded sufficiently by June 1862 that Phinney reported, "Freighting has rarely been better."[1] Why the turnaround? One reason was a series of combined army–navy coastal operations between September of 1861 and the spring of 1862 that neutralized havens of privateers and opened ports of the Chesapeake Bay, Carolinas and Gulf of Mexico to the coasters. Another was a new source of employment for them: war transport for the federal government. All the military, industrial and agricultural might of the North—troops, munitions, provisions, hay, coal, railroad iron—was worthless if it couldn't be gotten to the war fronts in the South. To get it there, the government chartered privately owned coasting schooners and other vessel types, many with Cape owners and crewmen.

The process by which a ship obtained a government charter, or "charter party," began with shipbrokers. In return for a commission fee, they passed on information regarding upcoming military expeditions and government ship needs to captains and owners who had listed their ships with them. A meeting would then take place. One can almost picture it: A dingy cubby hole of an office in a shed on a Boston wharf, a clerk or two perched on tall stools in front of high slant-top desks, stacks of ledger books on shelves behind. At the appointed time, the government quartermaster agent would appear. After a round of handshakes among agent, shipowner and ship captain and perhaps a few puffs of cigars, all would get down to the business of working out a price. Scenes such as this were frequent in the Boston office of Alpheus Hardy and Company and New York's Starks W. Lewis (both with Chatham connections).

The government paid handsomely to charter a large steamer. For example, the *Empire City* went for around $1,000.00 per day. A 1,000-ton, full-rigged ship might be worth several thousand dollars per month. Schooners were usually hired monthly and paid for by vessel weight. For instance, one month's hire of the 219-ton schooner *Charmer*, lying at Cotuit when chartered in March 1862, brought owner Owen Bearse $4.00 per ton or $876.00 total, money that was divided among himself, Captain Pardon Burlingame and the crew. At the low end, North Falmouth captain Thomas C. Lewis received just $15.00 per day for his 17-ton schooner *Reindeer*, acting as a lighter in South Carolina. Kickbacks, fraudulent representation of vessels and other improprieties tainted vessel chartering and led to several congressional investigations.[2]

It was a time of adaptation and improvisation. Steamships that had moved passengers between cities now moved troops to camp and battle. Clipper-type sailing ships that had transported fancy goods now hauled horses. Schooners formerly filled with flour hauled hay to feed the horses. And on board a great many of these vessels were Cape merchant seamen in their new roles.

1861

A number of Cape men did steady service the first year of the war on chartered steamships such as the *Ben Deford*, *S.R. Spaulding* and *Empire City*. Another steamship chartered that year was the *Chesapeake*. Diverted the first week of the war from commercial service between Portland, Maine and New York, she sailed from New York to Fortress Monroe, Virginia, under Captain Sidney Crowell of Hyannis, with barrels of provisions and a company of riflemen. In May, she transported cattle to Washington. In July, the steamer *Potomska*, normally plying between New York and New Bedford, went under charter to deliver ambulances for the government. A month later, she brought the crew of the captured privateer *York* from North Carolina to Fort Lafayette, New York, for imprisonment.[3]

One of the first Cape coasting schooners chartered was the *Western Star*, with George H. Crowell of Hyannis as master. In October, he transported coal, some in bags and some loose, from New York to Fortress Monroe. In December, he was at Port Royal harbor, South Carolina, loading government cotton, so designated because plantation owners had abandoned it in the fields when the area was captured. Also in December, the army quartermaster in Boston chartered the bark *Island City*—with David N. Kelley as captain—to convey 250 Confederate prisoners of war from Fort Warren (in Boston Harbor) to Fortress Monroe.[4]

THE DOORS OF RICHMOND

In January 1862, a huge assemblage of ships gathered at Hampton Roads, Virginia. Within was almost every class of ship imaginable, from tugs, barges and barks to ferryboats, schooners and steamships. This was the Burnside expedition, the same one in which Colonel Howard's marines participated. One of its vessels was the steamer *City of New York*, formerly of the Boston and Philadelphia Steamship Line and now commanded by Joseph Nye, who relinquished command of the *Potomska* when the navy purchased her in September 1861. Ward Eldridge was still his mate.

To reach the expedition destination of North Carolina's Pamlico Sound, Nye had to get his steamer across Hatteras Inlet's treacherous bar. Amid a gale and heavy surf, he approached and signaled for a pilot to lead him across. The pilot assured Nye he could do it, despite the vessel's substantial draft. Unfortunately, he miscalculated and the steamer lodged on shoals. In howling winds and raging currents, the stern-heavy steamer swung about, keeled over, capsized and broke apart. For some forty hours, the crew clung to the rigging, at times lashing themselves to it. Although Nye and his men

The wreck of *City of New York* on January 18, 1862. *Courtesy U.S. Army Heritage and Education Center.*

survived, the vessel and valuable barrels of powder, boxes of rifles and hand grenades were a total loss.[5]

Most of the expedition ships got across the bar safely, albeit with some tense moments. To brace up troops unaccustomed to Neptune's terrors, General Burnside came aboard the *S.R. Spaulding* and had Captain Howes run her up among the transports. At the sight of the general, soldiers cheered; ship captains blew steam whistles; and bands played "Home Sweet Home" and "Should Auld Acquaintance Be Forgot." Burnside made the *Spaulding* his headquarters vessel for the next phase of the expedition, the assault of Roanoke Island. After its capture, Benjamin Baxter visited the island and discovered, among the captured Confederates, five officers who had come down from Fort Warren on the *Island City* just weeks earlier! He expected they would soon see anew the inside of Fort Warren "or a kindred institution." While awaiting disposition, they received lavish accommodation on the *Spaulding*.[6]

While General Burnside probed the back door to Richmond in North Carolina, General George McClellan tried the front in Virginia in a spring 1862 offensive up a peninsula from Hampton Roads. Like Burnside, McClellan had massive waterborne logistical support, including six brigs and schooners with Cape captains. One was South Dennis captain Fernandus Kelley of the

The Attack on Roanoke Island, North Carolina, February 1862. *Courtesy U.S. Army Heritage and Education Center,*

Mountain Avenue. He knew the waters well, having sailed his schooner as a coasting vessel at Hampton Roads and nearby James River in 1860.[7]

With hard fighting in the campaign producing a mounting casualty list, the army converted the versatile *Spaulding* into a hospital ship. On May 22, 1862, a nurse on board described the process of loading the sick and wounded:

> *We are awakened in the middle of the night by a sharp steam whistle, and soon feel ourselves clawed by little tugs on either side of our big ship, and at once the process of taking on hundreds of men, many crazy with fever, begins. There's the bringing of the stretchers up the side ladder between the two boats, the stopping at the head of it, where the names and home addresses of all who can speak are written down, and their knapsacks…numbered and stacked. Then the placing of the stretchers on the deck…the lantern held over the hold, and the word given to "lower," the slow-moving ropes and pulleys, the arrival at the bottom, the lifting out of the sick man, and lifting onto his bed; and then the sudden change from cold, hunger and friendlessness to comfort and satisfaction winding up with his invariable verdict if he can speak, "this is just like home."* [8]

Also converted to hospital duty was the clipper-styled ship *Conquest*, chartered from Alpheus Hardy in August 1862. For Captain Winthrop Sears, who had captained passenger steamers and globe-circling clippers, this was a more sedentary employment, waiting off the quarantine station in lower New York harbor while sick and wounded on his ship were attended.[9]

THE BUTLER EXPEDITION

Ship Island, Mississippi—off the Mississippi River delta and designated as staging point for the campaign to capture New Orleans and reopen it as a port of the United States—underwent transformation in the winter and spring of 1861–1862 from nearly deserted sand spit to bustling military camp and stockpile. In command of the army phase of the combined army–navy campaign was General Benjamin Butler, who had recruited six New England regiments for it. The only means of transporting his six thousand men, horses and supplies down to Ship Island was the arduous one-thousand-mile sea voyage.

An important expedition troop transport was the chartered steamer *Constitution*. With nearly two thousand men on board, it awaited a favorable tide off Chatham on January 14, 1862, before continuing south. Three of those two thousand were Braddock Chase, Jonathan Burt and Charles Morrill of Waquoit, Hyannis and Wellfleet respectively, members of what would become the Thirtieth Massachusetts Regiment. Also chartered were four Alpheus Hardy vessels: in order of size, the ship *Ocean Pearl* and barks *Wild Gazelle*, *Young Turk* and *Daniel Webster*. All had Chatham captains: John Crowell, Thomas Sparrow, Samuel G. Harding and Richard Ryder respectively. Accusations swirled that horses transported on the *Pearl*, packed in "sweat boxes" in her hold, received inadequate ventilation. The five-hundred-ton *Wild Gazelle* delivered a long list of artillery pieces, ammunition wagons, brass guns, muskets and associated ordnance. Diverted from the Mediterranean fruit trade, the *Young Turk* transported provisions, among them spirits, for which Hardy received eighty-three cents per barrel.[10]

The ship *Idaho*, built and owned by Orleans relatives David and Josiah Snow Jr., carried troops. Her captain was an unidentified Howes. After running aground thirty miles short of Ship Island, the crew threw some eight hundred barrels of provisions overboard to lighten her. Two days later, she came free. Also getting a piece of the action was the former Boston–Galveston coasting bark *Thomas W. House*. Under instructions to house no more than ten officers in cabin accommodation and "suitably accommodate" one hundred men between decks, she transported troops. William Bearse was captain.[11]

PORT ROYAL AND CHARLESTON

Port Royal, the harbor at which George Crowell loaded cotton in December 1861, had been seized to provide the Union a base from which to bring the war to the Confederacy's southeast coastline. Still another army–navy strike force, this one supported by the steamers *Ben Deford*, *Empire City*, *Atlantic* and schooner *Virginia Price*, all with Cape captains, had wrested it from Confederate hands a month earlier.

Shortly after the harbor's capture, the steamer *Nuestra Señora de Regla*, just built in New York and on her way to Havana, Cuba, for service as a ferryboat, entered in quest of coal and was detained by military authorities. Several months later, Flag Officer Samuel Du Pont of the navy ordered Samuel Baxter of the *Empire City* to tow the *Señora* to New York for adjudication in the prize court. The navy purchased her, renamed her *Commodore Hull*, and placed the steamer in river duty in North Carolina where Harwich engineering officer Benjamin Bee served on her.[12]

The Transports

In November 1862, veteran Chatham shipmaster John A. Paine brought the chartered brig *Julia Ford* into Philadelphia Navy Yard from Port Royal. On board were 120 bales of cotton, on the final leg of a long journey from capture on the Texas coast to prize court in Philadelphia. A month later, cattle completed the final leg of a journey in the opposite direction, arriving at Port Royal on the brig *Benjamin Delano*, with Edwin Baxter of Hyannis as the captain. The animals had been transshipped on to the *Delano* at Hatteras Inlet after the steamer on which they began their journey in New York grounded in a gale. The editor of a Port Royal newspaper, grateful for the cattle's survival—and apparently anticipating some roast beef—penned, "The cattle are all fat and in good condition, seeming to have suffered very little. Praise be to Allah!"[13]

Gales imperiled man as well as beast on the voyage to Port Royal. All hands perished on the Cape schooners *Forest City* and *Howard*, bound there from New York with government stores in 1863. All of Osterville mourned the former since almost all her crew hailed from there. Fourteen from the community co-owned the vessel. The only remnants found from the *Howard* were gilt molding consisting of spread eagle, shield and coat of arms floating at sea and a trunk containing letters written to mate Harrison Bearse. A heavy load of cattle on the *Howard*'s upper deck may have put her in poor trim to endure a gale. All hands survived on a third Port Royal-bound Cape schooner to founder, the *Fannie Currie*. Allen Nickerson of Yarmouthport was captain.[14]

Close to the heart of a number of Union military planners was the capture of Charleston, that city north of Port Royal so central to the secession movement. As a first step toward that end, a fleet of troop transports left North Carolina for Port Royal in January 1863. Among them were the propeller-driven steamer *City of Bath* and the busy *S.R. Spaulding*. Captain of the *Bath* was Elisha Sears of Brewster. The attack began in earnest in July but bogged down and deteriorated into a siege, necessitating the deployment of big guns. The largest, a seventeen-thousand-pound Parrott rifled gun called the "Swamp Angel" because it was mounted in a salt marsh, had the range to send a shell over five miles into Charleston. Responsible for bringing the gun from its foundry in New York to South Carolina was Captain Sears; Abiathur Doane of Harwich assisted.[15]

To reinforce the Charleston offensive, the War Department ordered General George Gordon's three-thousand-man division from Virginia to Folly Island, an inhospitable strand south of the city. Within the division was the Fortieth Massachusetts Regiment with a contingent of Barnstable, Yarmouth and Sandwich soldiers. Both the *Empire City* and *S.R. Spaulding* conveyed troops. General Gordon, on the *Empire City*, even used Captain

Baxter's stateroom. After arrival near Charleston on August 13, Baxter anchored his steamer near the *Wabash*, flagship of the navy's South Atlantic Blockading Squadron. The next morning, he and the general's aide rowed to nearby Morris Island to find out the troop disembarkation plan.[16]

In February 1864, Captain Lyman B. Rich of Wellfleet transported horses from Washington to Port Royal in the schooner *E.M. Dyer*. Since the Fortieth Regiment became a cavalry unit around this time, Rich's schooner load may have furnished some of its mounts. In April, the War Department withdrew troops from the Charleston campaign and moved them to Virginia. A New York regiment came there on the steamer *Ranger*, with Nathaniel Bacon as the captain. So pleased were its officers with him, they thanked him publicly. When a Confederate army invaded Maryland in August 1864, General Ulysses Grant ordered a New York regiment north from Port Royal to help guard Washington. Bringing it there was the steamer *John Rice*, captained by Daniel Howes of Dennis. Vessel movement into and out of Port Royal was substantial throughout the war, and much of it had a Cape connection.[17]

VIRGINIA AND NORTH CAROLINA

Fully as important a destination for chartered vessels as Port Royal, and thus as instrumental in the Cape's 1862 economic turnabout, were various ports and landings along Virginia's James and York Rivers, and North Carolina ports of New Bern and Beaufort/Morehead City. Busily engaged in the James during the last half of the war was the steamer *Tillie*, captained by Henry Bourne of Sandwich. The steamer did not get off to a very good start in chartered service, however; she suffered a serious boiler explosion on January 11, 1863, off Sandy Hook, New Jersey, as she began a trip south with army stores.[18]

Government employment in Virginia kept several Cape shipmasters busy in May 1863. On May 2, Daniel Howes and the *John Rice* transported Confederate prisoners down the York River and, a few days later, Union troops up it. Meanwhile, John Orlando—four years removed from exoneration on his kidnapping charge and now with the schooner *Julia Smith*—conveyed railroad cars from Baltimore to Norfolk at the request of the U.S. Military Railroad.[19]

A year later, Union armies opened multifront spring offensives. One was an advance up the James River toward Richmond by the thirty-thousand-man army of General Benjamin Butler, no longer in the Gulf of Mexico. Conveying troops were the steamers *C.W. Thomas*, *Dudley Buck*, *Guide* and *Rockland*, all with Cape captains, mates or crewmen, as well as the *Ben Deford*,

Ranger and *S.R. Spaulding*. A supporting schooner was the *Avon*, commanded by Oliver Baker of West Dennis. Aboard transports was the Fortieth Massachusetts, just returned from its South Carolina service.[20]

Chartered vessels performed a variety of functions. For instance, after transporting troops up the James, the *C.W. Thomas* under Captain Edwin Doane of Harwichport became a flag of truce boat and spent the summer of 1864 moving Union prisoners of war from Bermuda Hundred down the James to Fortress Monroe and Confederate ones in the opposite direction. The assistant commissioner of prisoner exchange was a frequent passenger. In more conventional duty, the steamer *Guide*, with mates James F. Burgess and Benjamin Crocker Jr. of Brewster, brought reinforcements to Washington in July 1864, just as the *John Rice* had done.[21]

A Confederate stronghold that held out until the end of the war was Fort Fisher, at the mouth of the Cape Fear River in North Carolina. It fell, however, in early 1865 under massed Union land and sea power. Assisting was the steamer *Thames*, under Elbridge Arey of Wellfleet and Barnstable. On January 4, he picked up the 169th New York Regiment at Bermuda Hundred. Nine days later, it disembarked north of the fort, the first troops to come ashore in the assault.[22]

In end-of-war activities in the spring of 1865, Thomas Paine of Wellfleet brought anthracite coal from Philadelphia to Fortress Monroe in the schooner *S.A. Hammond*, while David N. Kelley, now in command of the *Abby Bursley*, received orders to proceed to the James River to be towed to the Washington arsenal. After the war, Confederate ordnance had to be collected and stockpiled. Accordingly, George W. Crowell transported boxed and loose muskets, mortar shells and six-and-a-half-inch solid shot in the schooner *E. Nickerson* from Richmond to Washington.[23]

BANKS EXPEDITIONS AND BEYOND

As 1862 progressed, Northerners saw usefulness in establishing a military presence in Texas. Such a presence might secure for Northeast textile mills, running low on cotton as they filled large and lucrative army cloth contracts, a needed new source of the staple. Further, it might induce Texas to return to the Union. Last, it might stop a flow of war supplies moving from Mexico through the Lone Star State to the rest of the Confederacy. Charged with establishing that presence was General Nathaniel Banks, former governor of Massachusetts. He and his twenty-thousand-man expedition left New

York and Hampton Roads for New Orleans in a fleet of steamers in early December 1862. A number of Massachusetts regiments were on the steamers, including the Thirty-eighth, with twenty-eight Falmouth soldiers; the Forty-seventh, with fourteen Brewster, Orleans, Provincetown, Sandwich and Yarmouth men on Rodney Baxter's *Mississippi*; and the Forty-first, with seven Cape soldiers, with Banks himself on the steamer *North Star*. The ever-in-motion *S.R. Spaulding* and *Empire City* were also part of the fleet. Conveying stores were the ships *Amazonian* and *Windermere*, captained respectively by Chatham shipmasters David E. Mayo and David J. Harding.[24]

In early 1863, New York shipowner R.L. Loper offered his new steamer *Exact*—"of great power, fast and safe"—for government charter. The government accepted his tender, and West Yarmouth ship captain Higgins Crowell took the steamer south. In September, he transported the First Vermont Battery from Louisiana to Sabine Pass, Texas, as part of an army–navy expedition to gain a foothold in Texas. The enemy, however, repelled the attack, and Crowell took his load of Vermonters back to Louisiana.[25]

In another attempt by Banks to plant the U.S. flag in Texas, the army and navy moved up the Red River of Louisiana in the spring of 1864; it was another failed expedition. On May 4, the steamer *John Warner* left Alexandria, Louisiana, retreating down river. Aboard was the Fifty-sixth Ohio Regiment, bound home for furlough, plus two hundred bales of cotton and seventy-six "unserviceable" horses. Two crewmen were Ebenezer Crowell, last heard from on the USS *South Carolina*, and Allen T. Chamberlain of Barnstable Village. Twenty miles below Alexandria, enemy forces ambushed the *Warner* from wooded riverbanks. In appalling carnage on the *Warner*'s deck, blood of dead and dying horses mingled with that of fallen men. Crowell and Chamberlain were taken prisoner but escaped by running through the woods until they were able to hail and board a passing navy gunboat. Theirs was one of most harrowing experiences of any of the Cape's transport sailors.[26]

Just after the war ended in 1865, fears of French imperialism in Mexico persuaded President Johnson to exercise the Monroe Doctrine and send fifty thousand troops to Texas. Accordingly, the *Exact*, with capacity for seven hundred men, awaited orders at Mobile. In June, the brig *Mystic*, under Horace N. Berry of West Harwich, transported railroad iron from New Orleans to Brazos Santiago at the mouth of the Rio Grande River. A month later, Edwin Baxter, still with the brig *Delano* but hauling hay instead of cattle, brought forage for cavalry and artillery horses to Indianola, Texas.[27] It was appropriate that Cape war transport activities ended where they began, at Indianola, the place of capture of the transport steamer *Star of the West* some four years earlier.

CHAPTER 5

HOME FRONT AND FRONT LINE, 1861–62

FIRST AID

In the fall of 1861, a group of New York City women, appalled by Europe's abysmal record on soldier care in the 1850s Crimean War and resolved the Union soldier have a better one, formed the United States Sanitary Commission. They publicized their organization, and before long, branches sprang up in communities throughout the North. Almost all of the towns and villages on the Cape had soldiers' aid groups, some associated with the commission and some independent of it. In homes and community halls Capewide, aid societies brought women together and gave them a sense of personal involvement in the war.

In October 1861, Eliza Phinney, wife of the *Patriot* editor, became president of Barnstable Village's society; Mary F. Scudder was its first secretary. That same month, Brewster's women organized themselves to knit socks for the soldiers. The "wide-awake ladies" of Truro collected and packed cornstarch, woolen drawers and quilts. In Falmouth, women *and* men pitched in. Men dug clams at Quissett, women prepared them and together they put on a "chowder" that raised over fifty dollars.[1]

Soldier benefits at Washington Hall in Chatham in November and December 1861 played to packed houses. Piano teacher Charles M. Upham led a "select" choir; Congregational minister Edward French offered a prayer; and another Congregational minister, Frederick Hebard of Harwichport, explained the workings of the sanitary commission. Patience Bearse of West Chatham assumed the vice-presidential duties of her town's aid society.[2]

The Glass Workers of Company I

Over thirty glassworks craftsmen were in the Sandwich company that went off to war in May 1861. Two months later, an officer of the Twentieth Massachusetts Regiment came to Sandwich and recruited six more. A few months later, glass blower Phillip Riley entered the New England Guards, predecessor of the Twenty-fourth Massachusetts Regiment. Thus, by fall, over forty glassworkers had enlisted—a glassworks labor force reduction so great that three of four furnaces had to be shut down and additional girls hired.[3]

The six glassworkers recruited into the Twentieth Massachusetts were assigned to the regiment's Company I. In October 1861, the Twentieth and other regiments crossed the Potomac River west of Washington to a cliff on the Virginia shore known as Balls Bluff where they found themselves pinned between the river and the enemy. The latter promptly attacked and drove the Union back. Benjamin Davis was fatally shot in the heart; Peter McKenna was killed while swimming the Potomac; and Thomas Hollis was wounded when his left index finger was shot off. Hollis had come to Sandwich from Birmingham, England, in 1856 at age nineteen. Davis was also from there. McKenna, the "pet and pride" of his captain, had worked at the glassworks from 1856 until his enlistment, giving all his five dollars per week wages to support his family with whom he lived.[4]

Another of the six, Terrence Murphy, developed severe, service-ending eye inflammation during the Virginia peninsula campaign. At the September 1862 Battle of Antietam in Maryland, Hollis, now the regimental color sergeant, was shot again. In the same battle, drummer Thomas Davis was shot through the lung and left for dead. Unable to move, he lay on the battlefield two days. Two comrades searched the fields near the Hagerstown Pike, found him and brought him to a hospital where he convalesced for four months. When able, he returned to Sandwich and received care from Dr. Jonathan Leonard. Davis's lungs, however, were never well enough to permit resumption of his old trade of glass blower. In December 1862, Ezekiel Woodward was shot dead in vicious street fighting at the Battle of Fredericksburg, making all six Company I glassworkers casualties of war.[5]

Soldiers Depart; Bodies Return

Benjamin S. Loveland, first from Harwich to enlist for three years, traveled south from Boston to Fortress Monroe with the Sandwich company on the *Cambridge* in May 1861. A resident of Boston at the time, he would eventually be in Company K of the Twenty-ninth Massachusetts. The first three-year enlistee from Truro was Boston student Richard T. Lombard, who entered the Sixteenth Regiment in June. First from Chatham was Charles H. Lyman, son of writing master Storrs Lyman.

The New England Guards were well-enough known that when its commander, Colonel Thomas Stevenson, advertised for volunteers in Cape newspapers in the fall of 1861, he attracted upward of twenty-five men. One was East Dennis's William Page, the first three-year enlistee from that town. Others were Riley of Sandwich Village and mariners Jesse Allen, Benjamin Ewer and John F. Fish of South Sandwich, all detailed as

Richard T. Lombard, Truro, Sixteenth Regiment, *Courtesy U.S. Army Heritage and Education Center.*

gunners on Captain Baker's gunboat *Pioneer* of the Burnside expedition. Another, Henry Ewer Jr., was a son of an insolvent Barnstable Village shoemaker who had died in the spring. Still another, Woods Hole farmer William S. Washburn, developed rheumatism from sleeping in the rain on swampy ground in North Carolina. At forty-four, he was perhaps a little old for a soldier's life. He and son George were the first of several Cape father–sons to serve.[6]

Also recruiting in the fall of 1861 was Captain James B. McPherson of the United States Engineers. Enlisting with him were five Cape men: James M. Baker of Harwich, David E. Cook of Provincetown, Atkins Higgins of Eastham, Sylvanus C. Hopkins and Benjamin C. Sparrow of Orleans. Most had been carpenters in civilian life. Sparrow gained further experience by assisting his father in removing salvage from ships wrecked off Nauset Beach and bringing it to Orleans by ox cart.

The forte of the engineers was building bridges. Promoted from privates to artificers, Baker and Sparrow helped build corduroy and pontoon ones. The Union retreat at Savage's Station on the Virginia peninsula in June 1862 kept their outfit busy destroying bridges it had constructed. While

24th Regiment.

NEW ENGLAND

GUARDS!

COMPANY I.

CAPT. J. L. STACKPOLE.

THIS Company is, with one exception, *nearly full* than any in the Regiment. Its ranks are filled, for the greater part, with good, respectable men from the interior of the State. But one third of its NON-COMMISSIONED OFFICERS are yet appointed; so that there is a better chance for active and intelligent men to see in it than there is elsewhere. It is hoped men may be found to make up its full number, here on the Cape.

Let men consider that every one of them is called upon to serve,—that it is one man's business as well as another's to help put down this overwhelming rebellion. Let them consider, moreover, that they provide as well for their families by going as by staying ; that they themselves are as well taken care of, and that their pay, State aid, &c., can all go to support those they leave behind.

Their PAY AND RATIONS commence when they enlist. From the time when they set down their names they may place themselves in the hands of the United States to be fed, clothed and transported, without further trouble or expense to themselves.

The EQUIPMENT furnished by the State,—which every man receives at once, is very liberal, including india rubber blankets, extra suit of under-clothing, towels, everything, in fact, necessary to comfort, besides the regular outfit.

Finally, GILMORE'S BAND is attached to the Regiment, giving it the best music in the service.

RECRUITING OFFICE

—AT—

BARNSTABLE,

—OPPOSITE THE—

Agricultural Hall.

JAMES A. PERKINS,

LIEUTENANT,
Barnstable, Oct. 8, 1861.

COMPANY B,

NEW ENGLAND

GUARD REGIMENT.

THE NEW ENGLAND GUARDS

Organized in 1812, and always occupying a first class position in the Militia of Massachusetts, were during the past winter re-organized as the

FOURTH BATTALION OF INFANTRY!

—AND—

UNDER THE COMMAND OF

Maj. T. G. Stevenson,

During their term of duty at *Fort Independence,* acquired a reputation for efficiency and drill second to none in the State.

MAJOR STEVENSON

Has received authority from His Excellency, JOHN A. ANDREW, to raise a

NEW ENGLAND GUARD REGIMENT !

This Regiment will be Officered in the best manner, and will consist of Picked Men.

D. JARVES,

Recruiting Officer at Sandwich.

Also, application may be made to S. B. PHINNEY, Barnstable. sept 10

List of Letters

REMAINING in the Post Office in Barnstable Sept. 7, 1861.
Julia E. Phinney, Owners of schr. Levant, Capt. Phinney, of schr Seneca, Betsey A. Witherell, John Collins, Elizabeth Whelan, Ely Sears, Thomas Clark, A. Percival, Capt. I. A. Howes, 2d, Hannah P. Bray.
E. JENKINS, P. M.
Barnstable, Sept. 7, 1861.   3w

Barnstable County Agricultural Society.

THE members of this Society are hereby notified to meet at UNION HALL BUILDING in Barnstable, on WEDNESDAY, the 9th day of October next, at ten o'clock A. M., to elect officers for the ensuing year, and transact any other business proper to be done at the annual meeting of said Society.
S. B. PHINNEY, Secretary.
Barnstable, Sept. 10, 1861.

September and October 1861 recruiting ads for New England guards. *Courtesy* Barnstable Patriot, *September 10 and October 8, 1861.*

George W. Wartrous, Harwich, Twenty-fourth Regiment. *Courtesy Harwich Historical Society.*

Atkins Higgins, Eastham, U.S. Engineers. *Courtesy Eastham Historical Society.*

thus engaged, enemy cavalry swooped down on them. "We took good aim and dropped several of them off their horses in fine style," reported Baker, showing that engineers could fire guns as well as bridges. "It was exciting times here last week, I tell you," continued the exhilarated Harwich engineer in a July 4 letter from the James River to his family.[7]

Several volunteers of the Sandwich company hailed from Barnstable. One was Barnstable Villager Martin S. Tinkham, who lived with his mother, Eliza. Separated from husband Richard, her sole means of financial support was her young son. Around September 15, 1861, Tinkham came down with typhoid fever at his unit's camp at Newport News, and two weeks later, he died. His captain, Charles Chipman, wrote the deceased's brother-in-law, Oliver Holmes, informing him he was sending the remains home packed in ice. The body reached Massachusetts before Chipman's letter so that the family, unaware Tinkham was even ill, received news unexpectedly by telegraph that his body would be arriving within the hour by train. Deprived of her son and his support, Eliza Tinkham scraped by during the rest of her days on the charity of friends and a small pension.[8]

Another Sandwich company volunteer who died in Virginia was John Weeks. Like Tinkham, commanding officers sent the body back, in Weeks's case to Pocasset. Of the three eldest sons of fisherman Willard Weeks and wife Eunice, all would serve, and two would die (John and Willard Jr.). Still another to die there was glassmaker William H. Wood. Deathly ill in January 1862, he had Captain Chipman write his wife, Phebe Wood. Not wanting to upset Phebe, thought to be in her "confinement," Chipman downplayed the seriousness of her husband's condition. Neither man knew she had already delivered. When Wood's remains reached Sandwich on January 23, stores closed and flags flew at half-mast. Coming home in February were the remains of David Blake, who had taught at a one-room school in North Sandwich. Severely kicked by a horse at the camp of his First Maine Cavalry unit, he had lingered several months before dying. His death left his widowed mother, Hannah, in "very trying circumstances" financially.[9]

Not much better off was Temperance Crocker of West Barnstable. Her son Asa went to the California gold fields in the clipper *Terror* in 1853. Three years later, her husband abandoned her, possibly for the Golden State. Then, her son Horace died in the camp of the Thirteenth Massachusetts in Virginia in February 1862. She had done what she could for him by contributing to West Barnstable's Soldiers Aid Group. Crocker's body was not returned but remained where he died. Also not returning was Braddock Chase. After gazing on his homeland as he went south on the *Constitution*—for the last time, as it turned out—he contracted illness at Ship Island, Mississippi, and died. A comrade had to write his last letter home. He was buried in Louisiana. The body of Truro's first-to-die—telegraph operator Edward Winslow—was brought home with funds voted by town selectmen.[10]

PROVINCETOWN DEFENSES

Relations between the United States and Britain soured at the end of 1861 when the captain of the Union navy ship *San Jacinto* ran down the privately owned British steamer *Trent* and had removed from it Confederate ministers James Mason and John Slidell. The British, seeing this as a flagrant violation of their maritime rights, demanded an apology and release of the ministers. To back up its demands, it sent troops to Canada. With war clouds gathering, Washington disavowed the actions of the *San Jacinto*'s captain and released the ministers (at Provincetown), quieting the situation and preventing war on a second front—a most unappealing prospect. All this saber rattling made Cape people imagine the state of affairs should a second-front foe capture Provincetown and its valuable harbor. "Suppose," wrote Phinney at the height of the crisis on December 17, 1861, "they [Great Britain] occupy the harbor and fortify High Hill and Indian Head or High Head, what ordinary force could dislodge them?" Rightfully concerned, Massachusetts and Cape officials began to agitate Washington for construction of fortifications at Provincetown and a military railroad out to them.

No bystander in all this, Provincetown held a "large and spirited" meeting on February 26, 1862, at which Eben S. Smith and Nathaniel E. Atwood were chosen as delegates to appear before a March congressional committee in Washington. Freeman Cobb of Brewster, Chester Snow of Harwich and Phinney also appeared. Washington, however, had more pressing needs than the Provincetown defenses, so no serious fortification action occurred.[11]

300,000 MEN

For the first half of 1862, the war for most Cape people was a distant, unintruding affair. This didn't mean, however, it wasn't closely followed. When victories came, they were celebrated with vigor. After the capture of Roanoke Island, North Carolina, by the Burnside expedition—with its forty or so Cape men spread among the Twenty-fourth Regiment, navy, marines and transports—Chatham's flags flew and guns roared while Barnstable Village's "old gun" on Cobb Hill thundered. Flags hoisted by Zoeth Snow Jr. and William W. Knowles demonstrated Brewster's patriotism.[12]

The Fourth of July brought reasons more than the day itself for celebration. The coasting industry had made a substantial recovery, and the upcoming mackerel season promised to be favorable. In the arc of foundries, tack, nail and marble factories extending from Sandwich Village around to Pocasset, business was steady. The glassworks were back in full production. Busily turning out woolen wares and "union cloth" for the army were the Robinson Mill at Waquoit and Pacific Mill at East Falmouth, the latter employing large numbers of both sexes. It could even be argued that the war had become a benefit.[13]

Testing that benefit, however, were events occurring elsewhere, rapidly catching the Cape in their clutches. With General McClellan's defeat on the Virginia peninsula forcing his hand, President Lincoln called for 300,000 troops to serve three years. Barnstable County's quota was 284, Sandwich's highest at 53 and Wellfleet's lowest at 3. The state adjutant general set the quotas, basing them on the number of enrolled militia (white male citizens ages eighteen to forty-five) submitted to him by town assessors' offices.

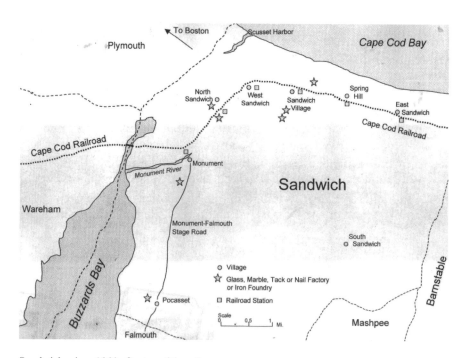

Sandwich, circa 1860. *Courtesy of the author.*

First to meet its quota and become the Cape's "banner town" was Provincetown. Responsible for this was the town's own Godfrey Rider Jr., who had been recruiting and advertising for the newly organized Massachusetts Thirty-third Regiment when the call for troops came. Having attended West Point, he had unusual credentials for a Cape Codder, a military background. Colonel Maggi of the Thirty-third promised Rider the adjutant position in the regiment. When, however, another man received it, prominent men of Provincetown wrote the governor in protest, contending Maggi sold the position. Rider and his sixteen volunteers left on July 21 for training at Camp Stanton at Lynnfield. They and their regiment left for the front a month later.[14]

A helpful recruiting tool for Rider was the state's twenty-five-dollar-bounty for each man who enlisted. Massachusetts officials had begun the bounty program in 1861 to encourage enlistment and also provide for a soldier's family in his absence. A further benefit, they reasoned, was a reduced desertion rate, since the soldier free of worry about his family was less likely to bolt for home. It was also hoped that bounties would prevent a draft—something no one wanted. Towns of Massachusetts tacked on additional bounty money. All thirteen Cape towns met in the summer of 1862 to hammer out the amount. Private citizens in Yarmouth, Dennis and other towns chipped in another twenty-five dollars per volunteer. When all was finalized, the average Cape bounty package in the summer of 1862 was around two hundred dollars.[15]

Godfrey Rider's recruiting ad. *Courtesy* Yarmouth Register, *July 11, 1862.*

Alvin Fish, Falmouth, Thirty-third Regiment.
Courtesy U.S. Army Heritage and Education Center.

Thirty-third enlistees from other towns included North Eastham farmer Nathan A. Gill, West Brewster men Alfred Twiss and John J. Ryder, West Falmouth laborer Benjamin Bowman and Hatchville brothers Alvin and Rufus Fish. The latter three enlisted at a New Bedford recruiting office of the Thirty-third. Ryder was fishing off the coast of Maine with Captain Valentine Newcomb when he heard about the call. Wishing to enlist, he asked his captain to bring him home. After landing at East Dennis, he signed up at Brewster as the first of the town's quota of five.[16]

A second Massachusetts regiment raised to meet the call was the Thirty-fifth. Surgeon George N. Munsell and two other men of Harwich reached Camp Stanton just in time to muster into it before it filled. Munsell, who had trained under Dr. Chauncey Hurlbert in South Dennis and graduated from Harvard Medical College in 1860, had just entered practice in Harwich. To reach the front near Washington, the Thirty-fifth had to pass through Philadelphia, a place that was notorious for liquor sellers proffering their wares to soldiers. The colonel of the regiment, after seeing his order forbidding sales of whiskey to his men was defied and his men were filling canteens with spirits, drew out his sword and smashed to pieces the booze bottles and glasses. "That," wrote Munsell, "proved him to be a man of worth."[17]

In Falmouth, a squad of thirty-one men loosely led by Elijah Swift left around August 15 for New Bedford, where he and his father had connections and Captain William Rodman was forming a company. Among the thirty-one were Swift's woodcutting cohorts Leonard Doty and James N. Parker. Several of the squad failed their medical examinations; Doty only passed by submitting to "a painful surgical operation." With their number reduced to twenty-eight, the men left on August 18 for Camp Stanton to join a third organizing regiment, the Thirty-eighth. Swift applied to the governor to be regimental quartermaster, citing his "special qualifications" of having supervised gangs of lumbermen in the South and lost property there to secessionists. He got the position.[18]

First to enlist at Chatham, and thus first of the town's quota of eleven, was its active minister Edward French, an 1859 graduate of Harvard Divinity School. Others in this rather colorful group were youngsters Daniel Ellis, William A. Gould and Roland Spencer (all around seventeen), Chatham villager Joseph Bloomer, North Chatham mariner Prince Eldridge, farmer Benjamin Batchelder and "senior statesmen" Eri Snow, Alvah Ryder and James Blauvelt. Forty-one-year-old Snow was a harness-maker. Ryder, old enough that he had gone to the California gold fields in 1849 with David Crowell, was evidently not feeling too old for a little more excitement. Then there was wheelwright Blauvelt of West Chatham, born in 1810! He had buried one wife, taken another and was supporting children of both. Two days after enlisting and three before leaving for Camp Stanton, he journeyed to Barnstable County Court House to execute his will. At the other extreme was Seth Howes, rejected from enlisting, apparently because he was too young.[19]

The eleven Chatham volunteers left for camp on August 1. Six took the stage from East Harwich to Yarmouthport, where driver Rufus Smith treated his passengers to breakfast at the Sears Hotel. At Boston, a son of Alpheus Hardy met those six—and the other five—and escorted them to Young's Hotel where Mr. Hardy himself furnished a "superb dinner." At the end of a busy day, they arrived at Lynnfield. Four Harwich enlistees—William Field, Asa Jones, Thomas Small and Henry Smalley—arrived around this time. All fifteen entered a fourth new regiment, the Thirty-ninth. After a month of drill and training, they received Springfield rifles and began to feel like soldiers. In early September, they and their regiment left for the front.[20]

Attorney and judge Joseph M. Day was instrumental in raising a company of forty-seven Barnstable and twelve Yarmouth volunteers, almost enough from each town to satisfy quotas. Day came to Barnstable in 1851, and in 1860, he was a delegate to the Republican national convention. Because he had recruited the company, he was elected its captain, which was the usual practice of the time. It didn't matter that he was untrained in soldiering. A few weeks later, the governor authorized an officer commission for Day, again the usual practice. Perceiving Day's lack of qualifications, volunteer Cyrus Fish of West Barnstable sneered—perhaps a little unfairly but undoubtedly accurately—"He don't know any more about military duty than I do."[21]

On August 4, two Barnstable volunteers for Day's company, Charles W. Crocker and William Lumbert, went from Hyannis to the courthouse at Barnstable Village, passed Dr. John M. Smith's examination, ate dinner

Charles W. Crocker, Barnstable, Fortieth Regiment. *Courtesy U.S. Army Heritage and Education Center.*

at Eldridge's Hotel and returned home. The next day, they and twenty-two other Barnstable volunteers took the "cars" to Boston, had dinner at Russell Marston's restaurant, reached Camp Stanton in the afternoon and, in the evening, partook of their first army meal, bread and coffee.[22]

First to volunteer from Yarmouth for Day's company was mariner Roland Lewis of South Yarmouth. Hearty cheering greeted him as he stepped upon the stage at a war meeting to sign his name. Vouching for his moral character and scholarly abilities was his grammar-school teacher. Lewis and the rest of Day's volunteers became part of Company E of the Fortieth Massachusetts Regiment. On August 25, Captain Day interrupted training of his company to return home to ceremonies at the courthouse, where colleagues of the bar presented him a sword, belt and field glass. Lending "soul-stirring" music to the occasion was the Sandwich band.[23]

Citizens gathered in Sandwich on July 22 to see about filling their quota. Selected to confer with the governor about raising a company of volunteers was the Reverend Frederick Freeman. When he announced the governor's decision to authorize the company at a packed July 26 meeting at town hall, cheers erupted, speeches emanated, cornets played, a glee club sang—and volunteers came forward. Among the first were boardinghouse keeper William H. Harper and Boston student Hartwell Freeman, son of the reverend. Tempering the excitement was the death of volunteer James G.B. Haines of Sandwich's first company, who had contracted typhoid fever in Virginia; he had come home sick on furlough and died at his home in East Sandwich, also on the 26th.[24]

Since Harper led the effort to recruit the new company, or second Sandwich company, as it was termed, he was elected its captain. Like Captain Day, he returned from camp for a presentation ceremony, in which citizens of Sandwich gave him a sword, sash and revolver in front of an "attentive audience" at the town hall. Hartwell Freeman was a lieutenant of the company. The new group of volunteers became the core of Company I of the

Fortieth Regiment. They, Company E and the rest of the Fortieth left on September 8 for Washington.[25]

The sixth and final three-year regiment formed in eastern Massachusetts in the summer of 1862 was the Forty-first. Some of its enlistees included sixteen-year-old Hyannis stepbrothers Andrew Cobb and James B. Ewer Jr.; Sandwich glassmakers Cornelius Dean, Edward Heffernan and James McKowen; and Theophilus Dill of Eastham. Cobb and Ewer joined Company C, headed by Captain John L. Swift, a Falmouth native. Heffernan left a widowed mother behind when he enlisted, and McKowen left a wife and two small children. The Thirty-third, Thirty-fifth, Thirty-ninth and Fortieth did much of their service in Virginia.

William H. Harper, Sandwich, Fortieth Regiment. *Courtesy U.S. Army Heritage and Education Center.*

Forty-first volunteers headed for Louisiana. *Courtesy University of Virginia Special Collections.*

John L. Swift, Falmouth, Forty-first Regiment/Third Cavalry. *Courtesy U.S. Army Heritage and Education Center.*

The Thirty-eighth and Forty-first went to Louisiana as part of the Banks Expedition.

They had done it! In an extraordinary summer on the Cape, hardworking selectmen, war committee members and recruiting officers had filled quotas and sent forth nearly two hundred volunteers to shoulder arms for three years in Union army regiments. Barnstable County was doing its part.

300,000 MORE

No sooner had the Cape responded to the summons for 300,000 three-year troops when a second call came for the same number for nine months' service. Looming over this call was the threat of a draft if the men didn't materialize; it was the first step toward national conscription in the North. Manpower on the Cape was beginning to dwindle. Sending more men "will drain Sandwich pretty well," wrote George L. Haines on August 17, noting that his town had already sent two hundred volunteers to the army.[26]

Governor Andrew began meeting this call by activating an old regiment, the Fifth, which had been inactive since 1861. Receiving a first lieutenant's commission in its Company E was Bostonian George Myrick, a Yarmouthport native. Possibly because of this, the company bore a strong stamp of that place. Isaac Myrick, foreman at the *Register* office, and Jarius Lincoln, principal at the grammar school, were sergeants. Edwin H. Lincoln, student of Jarius, was a drummer. Store clerks Darius Baker, E. Dexter Paine and David Snow were privates, as were bank clerk Franklin Thacher and saddler Charles P. Baker.[27]

Hyannis also had a large contingent in Company E. Brothers Alfred and Charles Finney, well-known because they drove a bakery wagon, were in its ranks as were butcher Thomas Eldridge, brick maker Ebenezer Eldridge and printer Lawrence Chase. From Dennis Village came carpenter

Edmund Matthews and farmers John W. Greenleaf, Jeremiah and Joseph Hall. Brewster sent six enlistees led informally by the patriotic Zoeth Snow, the first townsman to enlist in the second call. The Fifth trained at Camp Lander near Salem. Breaking camp early on October 22, it made a midday march down State Street in Boston. Banging away near the front of the column were the company drummers; one of them was Edwin Lincoln. At Battery Wharf, the Fifth boarded Rodney Baxter's *Mississippi* and sailed to North Carolina.[28]

Governor Andrew also authorized new regiments in order to meet the second call. Henry Doane left his legal practice in Boston to return home to Orleans to recruit a company for one, the Forty-third or "Tiger Regiment." Urging local men to "let the right arm of the Old Bay State be promptly raised," he attracted seventy-five volunteers from the Cape's elbow region. Their various communities extended expressions of appreciation as departure time neared. Orleans's citizens gave its enlistees a banquet. Brewster acknowledged its contingent in a rally at the Universalist Church. At Eastham's Methodist Meeting House, young ladies gave Bibles to the town's eight volunteers. Friends presented a revolver to volunteer Charles Upham at a reception at Chatham's Nauset Hotel. Harwich enlistee William H. Bassett attended to personal business, marrying Ellen

Darius Baker, Yarmouth, Fifth Regiment. *Courtesy U.S. Army Heritage and Education Center.*

2d Batalion of Infantry,

TIGER REGIMENT;

CAPT. CHARLES S. HOLBROOK.

The undersigned has been authorized to recruit a Company, to be attached to this favorite Regiment, for nine months service. This he proposes to do exclusively from the citizens of Cape Cod, thus affording friends and acquaintances an opportunity to march side by side to the rescue of the country. The Company will have the privilege of choosing officers from their own members, making it altogether a Cape institution. A fund is being raised for the benefit of the Regiment, and nothing will be wanting for its complete outfit and comfort in the field.

Sons of Cape Cod, rally on the Stars and Stripes and let the right arm of the Old Bay State be promptly raised to crush out this vile rebellion. HENRY DOANE.

Headquarters of the Company at Orleans.

Selectmen of towns in the County, and others interested in this movement are respectfully requested to corporate in the speedy enlistment of the company.

aug 26

Henry Doane's recruiting ad. *Courtesy Barnstable Patriot, August 26, 1862.*

Above left: Henry Doane, Orleans, Forty-third Regiment. *Courtesy U.S. Army Heritage and Education Center.*

Above right: George Nickerson, Orleans, Forty-third Regiment. *Courtesy U.S. Army Heritage and Education Center.*

Left: Joseph W. Paine, Wellfleet, Forty-third Regiment. *Courtesy U.S. Army Heritage and Education Center.*

Cahoon on September 9 in South Harwich. A day or so later, he exchanged conjugal duties for soldierly ones.[29]

On September 13, enlistees elected Doane as captain of the company, now designated Company E. Ten days later, he was in Orleans for the customary presentation, in his case "an elaborately finished" sword. George H. Nickerson of Orleans and Joseph W. Paine of Wellfleet were elected lieutenants, thus making Company E the only one of the war wherein all three officers were Cape Codders.[30]

Another new regiment was the Forty-fifth, also with a nickname, the "Cadet Regiment," because a number of its officers, including its commander, Colonel Charles R. Codman, had had an association with the Boston corps of cadets. Codman also had a Cotuit connection. Officers of the Cadets dispersed over the state seeking recruits. Lieutenant Cyrus A. Sears set up a recruiting station in Eldridge's Hotel while civilian Charles B. Hall, an apothecary, recruited in Sandwich. They enlisted around fifty men, all of whom entered Company D of the Forty-fifth, encamped at Readville.[31]

Prospective Forty-fifth recruit Eliphalet Doane of Marstons Mills flunked his medical examination because he was "minus" teeth. Determined to be successful in a second exam—or enter the navy if not—he obtained some artificial ones, paid for by the Town of Barnstable, and finally passed. Aaron H. Young's enlistment cost Barnstable Village the services of the Boston–Barnstable packet schooner *Mail*, of which he was master. In tidying up business affairs before leaving with the rest of Company D, he sold the little vessel. When he returned from camp on furlough in October, he also took care of personal affairs, executing his will.[32]

Like a lot of Cape men, George Haines agonized over enlisting. Tugging him one way were parents begging him not to go because they needed his care and had already sacrificed one son to the conflict. Tugging as hard on the other was the sight of schoolmates and comrades signing up and leaving without him and, in a broader sense, a feeling of wronging his country by not doing his part to defend it "in this unholy war." Once he decided to enlist, however, he was content, even when he learned that had he stayed with his countinghouse position at the Sandwich Glassworks he would have received a raise in pay to twelve dollars a week, compared to his private's pay of thirteen dollars a month. After settling into camp, Haines and his Company D comrades had Sandwich tinsmith Josiah Foster craft them a tin codfish, which they mounted like a weathervane on the flagstaff in front of their barracks to remind them of home and mark their quarters for visitors. Like the Fifth Regiment, the Forty-fifth went to North Carolina on Rodney Baxter's *Mississippi*.[33]

A final new regiment was the Forty-seventh Massachusetts. Entering it were seven men of Provincetown, four of them mariners, ship carpenters and caulkers of the maritime trades. A fifth was musician Caleb D. Smith, who retained that occupation after enlisting. The army's gain was Provincetown's loss—Smith had played his violin at most every dance in Provincetown.

From Yarmouthport came three men: carpenter Joseph Bassett, mariner John E. Ryder and of unknown occupation Benjamin Lovell. From Orleans came Azariah Walker. The Forty-seventh's service was in Louisiana.[34]

Barnstable County had done it again! On the heels of raising its quota of three-years' men, it had done the same with its nine-months' ones, through a combination of patriotic feeling, bounty money and revulsion at the idea of a draft. As the winter of 1862 arrived, more men of the county than at any time of the war had taken the field in the Union army.

ADJUSTMENTS AND ACCIDENTS

Answering the nation's call to enlist was one thing, adjusting to its realities quite another. Men of the Cape now began adapting to the soldier's life of drill, instruction, marching and occasional combat; digging, trenching and similar toil, known as fatigue duty, were also part of this new life. Thomas Wheeler Jr., a laborer in Sandwich in his preenlistment days but in March 1862 a private of the Twenty-eighth Massachusetts at Hilton Head, South Carolina, had no complaints about a little spade work: "I am at Work every Day Making Breastworks. I don't have to work very hard and I have 40 cents a day extary with my 13 Dollars a Mounth…It gives any one a good aptite…There is 2 hundred and 20 men Detailed every day."[35]

On the other hand, there were those who allegedly evaded work. Alonzo Bearse of Eastham contended that a comrade in the Forty-third Regiment, Joshua Small of Harwich, rubbed poison ivy on his arms and body so they would break out and get him out of doing duty. Bearse further maintained that when the unit got to North Carolina, Small drew up his right leg as if he had rheumatism and, because of it, never had to go on any marches.[36]

Soldiers could get hurt almost as easily in fatigue duty as in combat. Samuel Sampson of West Sandwich injured his back while unloading logs in December 1862 at the camp of his Fortieth Regiment at Miner's Hill, Virginia, near Washington. Artemus Young of Barnstable Village and the same regiment received a groin injury while erecting fortifications near the camp. A stick of timber fell on Lorenzo Drury of Hyannis while he was constructing rifle pits, breaking several ribs and knocking him senseless. Marching was also dangerous. Eri Snow was made to bear one end of a pole supporting three kettles filled with tea, sugar and coffee for a twelve-mile march in Maryland, leaving him utterly exhausted. A long march of the Thirty-third Regiment in Virginia in November prostrated Samuel Knowles of North Truro.[37]

Camp of Fortieth Regiment at Miner's Hill, Virginia. *Courtesy U.S. Army Heritage and Education Center.*

Soldiers also had to adjust to inspections. Drummer boy Edwin Lincoln wrote that fellow musicians of his Fifth Regiment "made a very poor appearance" during a November inspection at their North Carolina camp because "they have not had any instruction." He wrote "they" because he hadn't taken part—his drum had a hole in one of its heads. Also presenting a poor appearance was the food given the Forty-seventh Regiment while it camped on Long Island, New York, awaiting transport south. "We have on unquestionable authority," declared the chaplain, "that in the hash given to the boys on Saturday, potatoes were found with candle-ends in them, and undeniable traces of the ravages of rats." The food was in fact so offensive it provoked the men to create an unspecified "difficulty."[38]

Battles

Of the many places where Cape soldiers fought during the war, most remote was New Mexico. In the summer of 1861, Alfred S. Cobb of Brewster, living in the frontier town of Denver City in the Colorado Territory, received a lieutenant's commission and position of aide de camp to the commander of the First Regiment Colorado Volunteers. In a winter 1862 battle along the route of the Santa Fe Trail in Glorieta Pass, New Mexico Territory, the regiment defeated a Confederate force eyeing Colorado's gold fields. Had the Confederacy captured the mines, the outcome of the war could have been much different.[39]

Farther east a few months later, General McClellan's army battled its way up the peninsula of Virginia. After coming ever so close to Richmond, the

Confederate army counterattacked and began driving the Union toward the James River. On June 29, the retreating Federals had to abandon their field hospital and patients at Savage's Station to the enemy. In so doing, Private James H. Heald of Sandwich and the Twenty-ninth and engineer Benjamin Sparrow were captured. A day later, the Twenty-ninth and other units were assigned the task of protecting the rest of the Union army and its valuable wagon trains while they retreated through the farming crossroads of Glendale toward the river. This was its first significant assignment.

June 30 was a memorable day for the Twenty-ninth. Early that morning, its men assisted in destroying an important bridge over White Oak Swamp, after which they nervously awaited at Glendale the attack from the swamp of Stonewall Jackson's troops. Suddenly, Jackson's artillery opened up on them. All was pandemonium; several hundred mules, unhitched for watering, stampeded. "We had to look out both ways, being bombarded by Rebs in front and crazy mules in the rear," wrote Lieutenant Augustus D. Ayling of Company D. While his men lay on the ground, enduring "a horrible fire of shell, grape, canister, and apparently every known artillery projectile," a spent lead ball struck him on the arm but inflicted no injury. Beside him was Corporal Benjamin Hamlin, a glass trimmer in presoldier days. He picked the ball out of Ayling's blouse and gave it to his superior. "I shall keep it as a souvenir of White Oak Swamp, and a hard, nerve-wracking afternoon," wrote Ayling.[40]

In holding off Jackson at Glendale, the Twenty-ninth and rest of the Union rear guard denied the Confederates an opportunity to divide McClellan's army and bought it time to reach the James River and protecting cover of Union navy gunboats.

On July 17, Brewster native Charles Dillingham, most recently a clerk in Chelsea, enlisted in the Second Massachusetts Regiment. Just three weeks later, he and his unit charged across a central Virginia wheat field on the hot afternoon of August 9 in an attempt to drive the enemy from defensive positions in what was later called the Battle of Cedar Mountain. Wounded, Dillingham went by ambulance wagon to Fairfax Seminary Hospital, Virginia, where he died a month later. He is buried in the Alexandria, Virginia, Military Cemetery.[41]

On the offensive after Cedar Mountain, the Confederate army defeated the Federals on August 30 at the site of an 1861 Union defeat, Bull Run. Killed there were Isaac B. Crowell and Thomas Wheeler Jr. South Yarmouth-native Crowell had worked as a printer for the *Register*, and before enlistment, had moved to Marlboro to work for a paper there. His last breakfast was a mug of coffee and some crumbs of hard cracker. Wheeler had hoped he and his regiment would be on Boston Common on the Fourth of July 1862, celebrating the end of the war. Since the Confederates possessed the field at the end of the day, Crowell and Wheeler lie in nameless graves somewhere in Virginia.[42]

An emboldened Confederate army invaded Maryland, and on September 17 battled the Federals at Antietam. Cape casualties besides Thomas Hollis and Thomas Davis included David Coleman of the Twenty-ninth, who fought in the Union center at the Sunken Road, and Gilman Hook and Nathan Winslow of the Thirty-fifth, on the Union left. After a shell fragment struck the knee of West Barnstable harness maker Coleman, he was helped aboard the regimental surgeon's horse and led to the rear by the surgeon himself. Hook of West Harwich was thrown backward and stunned senseless by an exploding shell during the tumult of a charge by his regiment near the lower (Burnside) bridge. Soldiers trampled him, thinking he was dead; but he revived, crawled off the field, rejoined his unit and resumed combat. Winslow, married to Hannah Kelley of Centerville just five weeks before the battle, died of wounds in late November. Surgeon George Munsell labored three months after the battle at nearby Locust Springs's tented hospital.[43]

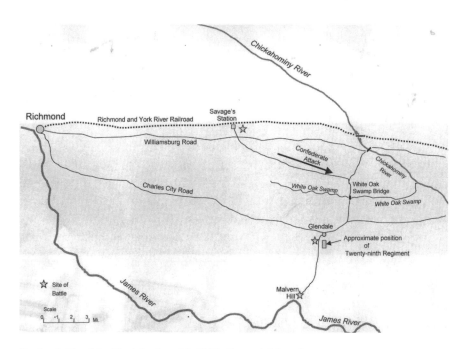

Battle of Glendale, Virginia, June 30, 1862. *Courtesy of the author.*

The Confederate army withdrew from Maryland after Antietam and in December Union forces attacked it at Fredericksburg, Virginia. In concert, General John G. Foster mounted an expedition from New Bern, North Carolina, to that state's interior to destroy rail communication with Virginia. Within the expedition were the Fifth, Forty-third and Forty-fifth Regiments that participated in battles at Kinston, White Hall and Goldsboro. At Kinston on December 14, the Forty-fifth made an assault through knee-high mud. In driving the enemy back, Clarence Bassett of Centerville, barely sixteen, was killed. Wounded by a rifle ball piercing his spine was West Sandwich blacksmith Henry Benson. He died two weeks later.[44]

At White Hall on December 16, the Forty-third encountered stiff opposition at a bridge. Pinned down by artillery fire, it could do little except find shelter behind trees and wait. An eight-pound solid shot carried off the left breast and right arm of Isaac Y. Smith of Orleans. Horatio Lewis of Chatham helped carry his lifeless comrade to the rear. "He was an excellent man and good soldier," wrote John W. Atwood, also of Chatham. A day later at Goldsboro, William E. Sparrow of Orleans was killed and Aaron H. Young badly wounded. Despite the casualties, Henry Knippe of Sandwich found the expedition exhilarating and regretted that his Forty-fifth would probably not see more: "I don't think we shall see any more Battles or tramps through mud up to your stern. Those times have gone past, but I enjoyed them."[45]

END OF YEAR AID

As more soldiers went off to war, aid activity increased. In East Dennis, Lydia Howes and others organized a society to work especially for Dennis's thirty volunteers. At Orleans, four sewing circles consolidated to form one aid group. In Harwich, nine women, including Cordelia Hall and Olivia Weeks, both in their teens, solicited aid. Eastham's ladies sent forward a box of miscellaneous articles. Stephen Wing, corresponding secretary of South Yarmouth's society, sent a box to which he added soldiers reading material, hopeful it "may tend while away a few tedious hours for the poor fellows." Barnstable County was pitching in, at home and in the field.[46]

CHAPTER 6

HOME FRONT AND FRONT LINE, 1863

LIFE HOME AND AWAY

New Year's Day 1863 in Falmouth seemed quiet, with large numbers of its young men away in the army. Heightening that sense was the arrival of letters from its men of the Thirty-eighth Regiment at far-off Ship Island, Mississippi. After spending Christmas on the island, the Thirty-eighth went up the Mississippi River to New Orleans, passing and exchanging greetings with Rodney Baxter's *Mississippi* with the Forty-seventh Massachusetts aboard. Back in Falmouth, a January 14 benefit at town hall raised money for soldiers through grab bags, "eatables" tables and "post office" run by twenty-three-year-old Sarah C. Lewis.[1]

In New Bern, a meningitis-like condition called "congestion fever" broke out in enlisted men but not officers of the Forty-fifth Regiment. Colonel Codman postulated that this might be because the officers received better food. George H. Bearse of Centerville died of the disease. Alfred Finney, at New Bern in the Fifth Regiment, wrote his mother in Hyannis on February 18 that all was quiet with "no news, as usual, in this department." He also asked how his father was managing in the family bakery business in the absence of him and his brother Charles. Three weeks later, Alfred was dead of the fever. Sound in body but not spirit was Warren H. Ellis, also of the Fifth. He wished he could be home in Yarmouth to go out in the morning and feed the hogs and hens. He hoped to send his mother enough money for her to buy a barrel of flour. Living at New Bern in conical tents, complete with furnace and kettle, were the men of the Forty-third. Sharing one such tent were fourteen men of Chatham, two of Orleans and one of

Truro. When Provincetown seaman John Powers of the Forty-third stole a haversack and canteen, he was sentenced to wear a barrel bearing the word "thief" in large letters.[2]

The assault of the Thirty-fifth Regiment at Antietam undid not only Gilman Hook but also Yarmouth soldier William H. Matthews. So overcome was he afterward, he had to be detailed to the Ambulance Corps, where he became quartermaster sergeant. In February, he died of typhus. Samuel Knowles's ailments continued after his company was transferred from Virginia to the Forty-first Regiment in Baton Rouge, forcing a stay at the camp hospital. While there, he received visits from comrade and North Truro neighbor Hezekiah Hughes. When measles broke out in the Forty-first in March, Falmouth soldier Joseph N. Landers contracted it. Thought to be recovering at the Measles Hospital near camp, he developed diphtheria and died. Comrades followed his remains to his grave where scripture was read over him.[3]

Early in its stay in Louisiana, the Forty-seventh Regiment did garrison duty at United States Barracks in lower New Orleans. When fever attacked Benjamin Lovell there, John E. Ryder helped him get to the hospital. Ryder also visited Joseph Bassett when he was hospitalized, showing this Yarmouthport threesome stuck together. Later in its stay, the regiment was at Metairie Race Course above the city. During a brigade review there, soldiers had to leap a ditch. In so doing, Azariah Walker, apparently not as agile as some, tripped and injured his spine. More "agile" was Yarmouth seaman and Fortieth soldier Freeman Cash. While home on furlough, he deserted, which was a capital offence. Edwin Bearse of Hyannis had no sympathy for his Company E comrade, as Cash's misconduct made it more difficult for others to get furloughs. "I would be glad to see him shot," he wrote.[4]

FIGHTS AND FORAGES

The Confederates were not inactive while the Fifth, Forty-third and Forty-fifth were at New Bern. In late March, they laid siege to Washington, a garrisoned town forty miles to the north, and placed batteries along the Tar River to prevent its resupply. On April 14, Francis Tripp of Dennisport and others of Company E, Forty-third, volunteered to run past the batteries at night in a supply-filled schooner. Withstanding fierce sharpshooter and artillery fire, they made it. A few days later, he and others volunteered to investigate a report from deserters that the enemy had evacuated its works.

Unfortunately, the report was inaccurate, the party was ambushed and Tripp took a bullet in the abdomen. He and his cohorts only escaped by jumping into the river. Tripp carried his lead souvenir, festering in his groin, for the next thirty years.[5]

In a move to take pressure off embattled Union forces along Virginia's Nansemond River (where pilot John W. Small had been wounded), the Forty-fifth Regiment climbed onto open railroad cars and rode west on the tracks from New Bern to Gum Swamp where it overran an inferior enemy force. After George Haines helped plant the regimental colors, he looked at some dead Confederates and reflected, "What a curse this war is. It is just like shooting down our own citizens."[6]

In May, the Union's Army of the Potomac had a new commander in place of McClellan, Joseph Hooker. Cyrus Fish had confidence in him. "I am in hopes to see richmond before long. Gen Hooker is going to open the way and we are going to follow him," he wrote from West Point, Virginia, where his Fortieth Regiment, in General Gordon's Division, had been sent in hopes it would divert enemy troops from Hooker. Fish badly misjudged Hooker, who was soundly beaten at Chancellorsville.[7]

This notwithstanding, Fish liked West Point "first rate." Whereas at the Fortieth's camp at Miner's Hill he had drill, here he had none, plus he had the excitement of being on a foraging crew in a rich farming area. "We hav [sic] plenty of milk for we can catch a cow most any time." If farmers refused to sell their livestock, the foragers helped themselves, justifying their actions on the fact that "the folks are all rebs." Fish killed four pigs with his bayonet. His Cotuit neighbor, Abijah Baker, found West Point less likeable. He contracted typhoid fever while doing picket duty in the Chickahominy River Swamp and had to take a medical discharge.[8]

FATHER OF WATERS AND MORE

All that remained in the spring of 1863 to opening the Mississippi River was elimination of enemy strongholds at Vicksburg, Mississippi, and Port Hudson, Louisiana. In a flanking move to reach the rear of Vicksburg, the Yazoo Pass Expedition blasted levees and flooded tributaries, but enemy defenses—including Elisha Howes's *Star of the West*, now sunken in the· Tallahatchie River—foiled the plan. This unsuccessful—and unhealthful—enterprise cost Andrew T. Shiverick his life. He died in a Memphis hospital on April 22.

Andrew Shiverick, Falmouth, Twenty-eighth Wisconsin. *Courtesy Woods Hole Historical Collection.*

Shiverick had gone to Milwaukee after graduating from Yale and joined the Twentieth-eighth Wisconsin Regiment, led by his uncle James M. Lewis, formerly of Falmouth, now a physician and, as a colonel, one of the higher-ranking Cape-born officers of the war. Shiverick served under Lewis as a company commander. The diary entry of Maria Jones for the evening of May 2 closes this sad story: "Did some shopping at New Bedford, took the boat [steamer *Monohansett*] for home, Andrew Shiverick and Celia were on board with the corpse of their son Andrew who died out west of fever." Young Shiverick is buried in Falmouth's Oak Grove Cemetery.[9]

While Grant campaigned against Vicksburg, Banks moved his army north from New Orleans against Port Hudson. Two of his divisions (the Thirty-eighth Regiment within one) marched there over an arduous swamp route west of the Mississippi. Unable to slog farther, Cornelius Fish of Falmouth fell out of the ranks on April 14 with swollen leg veins. Visiting him at the Brashear City, Louisiana hospital was his friend from childhood, Elijah Swift, now brigade quartermaster.[10]

Banks's army besieged Port Hudson. In a June 14 assault, Augustus Foster of East Falmouth was shot. He died a week later, the only Cape combat death of the siege. A noncombat one was farmer Jehiel Fish, brother of Cornelius, who died of disease. Jehiel's loss was severe for his mother Pamelia, in part because he had been supporting her. Expressman William Hewins, who drove the Monument–Falmouth stage, knew of his support because he had delivered a package to her from Jehiel containing twelve dollars. Henry O. Davis of Falmouth, a clerk as a civilian, served as an orderly for General Emory during the siege. A few days before Port Hudson surrendered on July 7, finally opening the Mississippi, quartermaster Swift was captured at the Union supply base of Springfield Landing. After being held prisoner at Liberty, Mississippi, most of July, he made his way back to safety with a Union infantry force that had penetrated interior Mississippi.[11]

Joining Higgins Crowell and the *Exact* at the Sabine Pass, Texas Expedition in September was the navy steamer *Sachem*. Serving aboard as signalman was Andrew P. Cobb, detached from his Forty-first Regiment. While wigwagging other ships from an exposed position on the deck, a shell struck the *Sachem*'s boiler, releasing steam and scalding him to death. Comrades had to leave his body on deck because the *Sachem* was captured. Cobb's widowed mother in Hyannis mourned his death many years.[12]

Elijah Swift, Falmouth, Thirty-eighth Regiment. *Courtesy U.S. Army Heritage and Education Center.*

COMINGS AND GOINGS

The nine-months regiments returned from North Carolina and Louisiana in June and July. A party of well-wishers from Brewster traveled to Yarmouthport depot to escort home its returnees of the Fifth Regiment. Although the assemblage reached Brewster late at night, this didn't stop residents from illuminating windows of houses and shops in welcome. Many residents, however, did nothing. "I am ashamed of Brewster," wrote dress and hat maker Martha Huckins. "All the patriotism in it could be held in your hand. Only a few care." In ceremonies the next day, men of the town botched giving "three cheers" for the returnees. "I think the men of Brewster had better get together and practice cheering," jested Huckins. "If not, the ladies will take it out of their hands." Meanwhile, private school teacher Clara Baker solicited soldier's aid.[13]

The able-bodied men of the Forty-third Regiment left New Bern on June 24 on transports for Boston, leaving behind Francis Rogers of Chatham and other sick men. "Everything quiet since the Reg left," he wrote July 4. A day later, the sick of the Forty-third and two other regiments—150 ambulatory and 100 on cots—left for the North on the transport vessel *Convoy*. Rogers was well enough to attend them during the voyage. His vessel passed Chatham in thick fog at 4:00 p.m. on July 9.[14]

In charge of the Forty-third's sick on the *Convoy* was Lieutenant George Nickerson. After arrival in Boston, he took those hailing from the Cape to their homes. Henry Doane, Charles Upham, John W. Atwood, William Harley, Franklin Hammond and others of the Forty-third volunteered to delay their return a month to do provost duty in Harpers Ferry. Through the efforts of Lieutenant Joseph Paine, around fifteen Cape men of the Forty-third reenlisted in the Second Massachusetts Heavy Artillery, also at New Bern. Those men received bonuses, immediate discharge from the Forty-third and thirty days' furlough.[15]

Reenlisting in a different way was twenty-three-year-old Asa S. Jones of the Thirty-ninth Regiment. In August, he applied to be examined for an officer position in the colored troops. Approved for that and recommended by the colonel of the regiment, he became a lieutenant in the Sixth U.S. Colored Troops. Jones's father had died around 1845, after which his mother Love married South Harwich cooper John B. Tuttle. In September, Adaline Knowles of Orleans asked the governor "in the interest of befriending the widow and the fatherless" (her husband died in 1851) to grant son Alfred a commission, as it had been learned the governor was seeking able noncommissioned officers for officer positions. Knowles became a lieutenant in the black Fifty-fourth Regiment. He, Jones, two sons of Sandwich ministers (Hartwell Freeman and Giles M. Pease) and three other Cape soldiers received officer positions in black units.[16]

GETTYSBURG

At the three-day July 1 to 3 Battle of Gettysburg, the Second Massachusetts Regiment arrived the first day but saw little action until the morning of the 3rd, when it was ordered to charge a fortified position near Spangler

Spring at the north end of the Union line. In this action, Samuel T. Alton of Sandwich was shot "dangerously" in the left thigh. He died seventeen days later at the Twelfth Ambulance Corps Hospital. The Eleventh Massachusetts reached the battlefield early on July 2 and, later that day, charged a strong position near the south end of the line. In this fight, Colin Shaw, brother-in-law of Alton, was shot, also in the thigh. He was admitted to Catholic Church and Seminary Hospital at Gettysburg on July 3 and died August 6. Alton and Shaw, the only Cape soldiers to die from the battle, have adjacent stones at Sandwich's Mount Hope Cemetery.[17]

Also at Gettysburg were the Fifth and Ninth Massachusetts Light Artilleries, or Batteries. Joseph Alton, brother of Samuel, was with the Fifth and George F.W. Haines of East Dennis, a native of Sandwich and cousin of James and George L., was with the Ninth. Three pairs of horses pulled a Civil War cannon and its wheeled accessories, a limber and caisson. Haines's task with the Ninth was to ride one of the center pair of horses when the battery was moving and hold the horses at the rear when it was stationary. As the battery took casualties, he would be expected to perform other tasks.[18]

The Fifth and Ninth Batteries saw intense action the second afternoon at Gettysburg near where Shaw was wounded. At first, they inflicted heavy damage on the enemy. Later, however, opposition infantry overran them and forced a retreat, costing the Ninth a number of men and four of its six guns. Enemy artillery fire that was overshot killed many of its horses, probably some of the ones Haines would have been holding. Sharpshooters

Dead horses of Ninth Battery Gettysburg. *Courtesy National Archives.*

killed others. A photograph of these dead animals is one of the more searing images of the war.[19]

Pursuing Lee's retreating Gettysburg army, the Fortieth Regiment marched seventeen miles through Maryland on July 15. The next day, it helped bridge the Potomac at Berlin (Brunswick), Maryland. Later that day, weary Barnstable Village harness maker William D. Holmes succinctly recorded in his diary, "Had a drink of Whisky."[20]

ILLNESS

Cyrus Fish wrote from Virginia on August 5 that his health was good and that of tent mates Stephen Jones of Marstons Mills and William Gifford of Cotuit, "smart" as he put it. Two days later, they and their Fortieth Regiment left for Folly Island, South Carolina—a "God-forsaken place" in the words of Barnstable Villager Winsor Nickerson, who tented there with William Holmes and Joseph Holway. The health of the Fortieth suffered greatly on this barrier island. A steady diet of hard bread, salt beef and pork led to cases of scurvy. Noah Bradford of Hyannis lost his teeth because of it. Many men had intestinal disease. The regimental hospital was of little help, as it was no more than a tent with room for but twelve patients. Many sick men languished in their quarters.[21]

Nathan Pitcher died on November 14; Samuel Otis died on the 16th; and Obed Cahoon died on the 21st. The regimental surgeon wrote that he would endeavor to have the grave of Pitcher, a Hyannis soldier, "well marked." Otis had worked several years at the *Patriot* office. Cahoon was from Cotuit. Just before Christmas, the *Patriot* urged readers to remember its men of the Fortieth and send them their greatest needs, jellies, preserves, cordials and woolen clothing. A comrade wrote the last letters of mortally ill Luther Hammond of Monument, sending them to his sister Eliza Wright. After Hammond died on Christmas Day, the comrade wrote Wright that her brother was buried with military honors; the American flag was draped over his coffin; and the body could be sent home if a friend came to claim it.[22]

James H. Baker of the Thirty-eighth Regiment and East Falmouth was discharged in August in Louisiana because of chronic disease. A son of village postmaster Elnathan Baker, he failed to recover after returning home and died in November.[23]

THE DRAFT

To obtain its summer 1863 manpower needs, the War Department instituted the draft. In Massachusetts, no new regiments formed except the black Fifty-fourth and Fifty-fifth. Drafted white men faced the unappealing prospect of entering regiments of strangers and hard-core veterans. War-weariness was also settling over the North. To avoid service, draftees throughout the state—the Cape included—furnished substitutes and paid commutation fees when medical, family and alien exemptions failed to disqualify them. Of 914 Barnstable Countians drafted, just 7 were enlisted into service: Nathan Jenkins of East Falmouth, Edward Holway of East Sandwich, Thomas F. Crocker of West Barnstable, Charles L. Ellis of Hyannis, William Branch of South Dennis, Josiah C. Freeman of Orleans and Henry A.F. Smith of Provincetown. Albert H. Lawrence of Falmouth was a substitute for draftee William H. Garrison of Harwich; Abraham Berry one for fellow Brewsterite Theophilus Harding; and John H. Cowan one for fellow Orleansian Charles H. Snow. Scotsman Cowan's alien status exempted him in the draft but not in being a substitute.[24]

Jenkins, working in Joshua Robinson's country store when drafted, went with the substitutes and other enlisted draftees to a special camp on Long Island in Boston harbor where conscripts were confined like convicts and from which many tried to escape. Gustavus C. Robbins and Ezra Kelley of Harwich did guard duty. Godfrey Rider and a detail of men of his Thirty-third Regiment came to Boston from Virginia to obtain men from the camp, as did Charles Crocker of the Fortieth. A passenger on the Boston–Provincetown steamer *George Shattuck* commented that the route ran past Long Island "covered with the white tents of the conscripts."[25]

In August, Jenkins went south to Virginia on a steamer. He may have been on the *DeMolay*, on which conscripts tried leaping overboard and setting fire to the vessel to get free. Writing of his voyage, Jenkins related, "We had a hard time comeing [*sic*] as there was such a hard set of Boys they robed almost everyone on board." He resolved to make the best of his involuntary service. "[I] am going to do my duty like a man. I left home like one and if I ever return it will be like one." Four months later, he died at a Confederate war prison.[26]

African American Ellis moved from Sandwich to Hyannis in 1860 and went into business as a barber. In 1862, he rented rooms at Yarmouthport's hotel where he followed his trade twice a week. He was mustered into the Fifty-fourth Regiment and served two years. His wife "took up" with another man on account of her husband's having gone to war. Ellis and George H. Clark of Sandwich are the Cape's only known African American soldiers of the war. Quaker Edward Holway refused to serve after he was enlisted and was discharged.[27]

The War Department made another call for 300,000 troops in mid-October. Bounties were offered in this call, something Governor Andrew had wanted in the summer but which Washington had refused; the bounty was now sweetened to $727 for veterans, $627 for new recruits. Towns had until January 6, 1864, to fill quotas through bounties, with deficiencies thereafter made up through the draft and bounties suspended. Men who failed to volunteer risked being drafted and losing sizeable bounty money. Barnstable's quota was a hefty sixty-two men, Dennis's fifty-two and Harwich's fifty. Horatio Lewis, who had received a lieutenant's commission, opened a recruiting office in the White House Hotel in Hyannis while Charles Upham, just promoted to first lieutenant, manned one at Washington Hall in Chatham. Harwich's selectmen established one in the town almshouse. Rawlins T. Atkins, serving since the start of the war in the First Massachusetts, left that unit with an officer's commission to recruit in Provincetown. Volunteer Charles W. Hamilton, formerly a seaman, addressed war meetings in Harwich's Exchange Hall. At a largely attended one on Saturday night, December 19, half the audience was women.[28]

A widely held sentiment in the North at the end of 1863 was that the Confederacy, after defeats at Gettysburg, Vicksburg and Chattanooga, was nearing collapse. In weighing volunteering, Ebenezer Smalley of Harwich likened its state to "a great boulder teetering on the edge of a cliff. Perhaps a few more good Cape Cod shoulders to the stone and over she will go." How accurate was his assessment? Time would tell.[29]

CHAPTER 7

HOME FRONT AND FRONT LINE, 1864–65

REGIMENTS NEW AND OLD

Provincetown brought in 1864 with a bang, as revealed through John E. Smith's diary entry of January 5: "All the volunteers marched in rank through town. Bunting flying from one end to the other. Cannon used. In evening marched on the Hill with drums and flags. Received the news that quota filled." Not only had Provincetown met its quota of forty-three, it had done it with local men. "Not one man bought in Boston," proclaimed the correspondent of the *Patriot*. Most of the forty-three, Smith included, entered Company H of the new Fifty-sixth Regiment. The remainder joined the old Forty-first Regiment/Third Cavalry in Louisiana.[1]

Equaling Provincetown's success were Chatham and Harwich, where around thirty men of each town nearly filled quotas. Those volunteers entered Company A of the new Fifty-eighth Regiment. Charles Upham, elected captain of the company, had come a long way from his not-so-long-ago days as a music teacher. His men bought him a sword, and Nathaniel Smith of Chatham presented it to him. The key to recruiting success in Provincetown and Chatham/Harwich was the work of local veterans, with Rawlins Atkins in the former and Upham the latter. Other towns, in contrast, lacking a local veteran to recruit, had difficulty luring their men, even with bounties. Orleans, for example, attracted but two; the rest of its quota of nineteen were "aliens." What seems to have happened is that men subject to draft paid their commutation fee and that was used to hire recruits from off Cape. The Cape lost the effective recruiting services of Horatio Lewis when he was found intoxicated at Readville and left the service.[2]

John E. Smith, Provincetown, Fifty-sixth Regiment. *Courtesy U.S. Army Heritage and Education Center.*

Rawlins T. Atkins, Provincetown, Fifty-sixth Regiment. *Courtesy U.S. Army Heritage and Education Center.*

Five men of Truro were in Company A of the Fifty-eighth. One, Benjamin K. Lombard, wrote his sister Sarah from Readville in January that he liked camp and comrades: "We have got a nice set in our company for they are all Cape boys." In a February 26 letter, he offered her some brotherly encouragement, mindful that Leap Day was nearing and, at twenty-four, she was still unmarried: "Sarah! Please remember that it is leap year and take courage, for there never was a goose too gray." Liking camp perhaps less, Fifty-eighth recruits Thomas Coleman Jr. and Allen Marchant overstayed furloughs in Hyannis, were arrested by Barnstable war committeeman Joseph R. Hall and sent back.[3]

Units training at Readville had high regard for General Burnside, who reviewed them February 4. "Wee expect to go out with Burnside and I hope wee shall," wrote Simeon C. Childs Jr. of Marstons Mills and the new Fourteenth Battery. "He is a noble looking Gen.," recorded Smith, who came to Provincetown a day later to recruit for his Fifty-sixth Regiment, setting up an office at Seth Nickerson's store. On February 14, the regiment's

Band of Fifty-sixth Regiment. John E. Smith may be second row, third from right. *Courtesy U.S. Army Heritage and Education Center.*

twenty-two-piece band arrived to assist. February 20 was a big day; bugler Smith and the band took stages to Wellfleet, paraded through town and, after some initial objections, performed at the M.E. Church. Afterward, they serenaded the town, visited the ice cream saloon, serenaded Truro and at 2:00 a.m. returned to Provincetown and burst into still more serenading. "Very generous in their thanks" were the roused residents—according to Smith. Although unsuccessful in recruiting in Truro and Wellfleet, he attracted ten in Provincetown.[4]

Recruiting continued in Harwich, where war meetings brought out large turnouts of "ladies." There was discussion of moving the traditional Saturday night meetings to another evening since Saturday was baking day and "the women folks would be rather tired." Meetings in March procured ten recruits for Company H of the Fifty-eighth. William Harley became captain.[5]

To the Front

The Provincetown Ladies Relief Society gave each of the town's volunteers in the Fifty-sixth a parting gift, a compact called a "housewife" filled with sewing items for use in the army. They would need every such refinement because choirboys this regiment was not. On March 19, the day before the regiment departed for the South, thirty gallons of whiskey were confiscated from persons coming to see the men off. In Philadelphia, the whiskey sellers were out, and Colonel Weld of the regiment had to demolish one of their liquor shops. At Annapolis, where it camped for a month, a private had to be tied up by his thumbs for drinking, and Smith had "a pretty smart row" with tent mate Taylor Small Jr. for drinking up all his whiskey. Other tent mates were Jesse Freeman Jr., Robert Hooten and brother Freeman.[6]

As Childs had hoped, his Fourteenth Battery was attached to General Burnside's Ninth Corps. Also attached was the Fifty-sixth. On April 9, Burnside ordered it vaccinated for smallpox. Four days later, he and General Grant reviewed it and other regiments. To the eyes of Weld, Grant appeared "anything but able-looking." A more impressed Smith commented, "Grant does look splendid." The band serenaded and may have played for the generals its new number, "Nightingale Polka."[7]

Between April 23 and May 4, the Fifty-sixth marched eighty miles from Annapolis to the front at the Rapidan River in Virginia. The first day's march covered twenty miles. "I stood it 15 miles, then taken sick and fell out 7 times," wrote a wearied Smith. The quartermaster sergeant had to put him in the baggage wagon. Also falling out was nineteen-year-old seaman Samuel Pettes. Seaman Joseph King was detailed to the Ambulance Corps. Footsore Smith did better on April 24. The next day, the regiment marched on Pennsylvania Avenue, past the reviewing eyes of President Lincoln. On

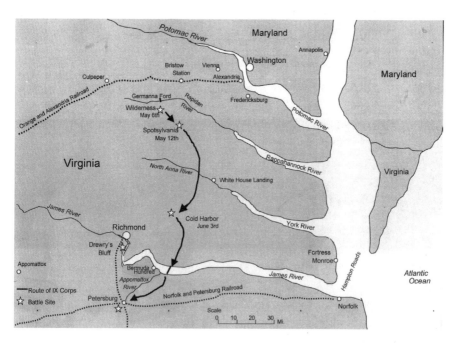

Map of Civil War-era Virginia, 1864. *Courtesy of the author.*

May 5, it covered thirty miles, a stretch Smith called the "hardest march I have ever known." At the end of this grueling day, it crossed the Rapidan on a pontoon at Germanna Ford and waited, expecting to be attacked. "The whole Army of the Potomac is on the move," wrote Sergeant Joseph J. Rudolph of Wellfleet, a veteran in the Massachusetts Twelfth Regiment. "The army is now getting ready for the grand struggle of victory."[8]

The Fifty-eighth left Massachusetts on April 28. After reaching Alexandria, Virginia, on May 2, it took the train to Bristow Station near Manassas where it spent an inauspicious first night in the field camped in the rain, causing many men—Charles W. Hamilton among them—to come down with illness. Here the regiment was assigned to the same corps as the Fifty-sixth but different division. Over the next few days, the men marched some forty miles, their first hard marches. When Aaron Snow of Chatham fell ill on the May 4 march, Captain Upham detailed Washington Eldridge, also of Chatham, to stay with him until he could catch up; John B. Tuttle also sickened. Alonzo Rogers Jr. of Brewster and Benjamin Lombard made a pact to look out for each other in case of wounds or sickness. When Rogers fell out with sunstroke, Lombard remained behind with him and was captured. Also getting captured by falling out was Lombard's Truro neighbor John C. Ryder. Like the Fifty-sixth, the Fifty-eighth on May 5 crossed at Germanna. All the horrors of war lay before both.[9]

FOUR BATTLES

May 6, 1864, was a grim day for the Cape. Just eight days after leaving Massachusetts, the largely green Fifty-eighth went up against battle-hardened Confederates at the Battle of the Wilderness. Considering its inexperience, it performed well. In fact, if Burnside had provided better leadership, the regiment and other units might have broken enemy lines. Killed was seventeen-year-old Seth Howes, who was too young in 1862 to enlist; since then, he had supported his family with wages from fishing voyages to the Grand Banks. Harwich soldiers Tuttle, David P. Ryder and Stephen Smith went into battle together but only Tuttle and Ryder came out. Smith, never seen again, left a widow and several children. Mortally wounded were Simeon Cahoon, Samuel Maker, David Young, John A. Nicholson of the Fifty-sixth and substitute John H. Cowan of the Fifteenth. A musket ball shattered the upper left arm of Yarmouthport and Fifty-eighth soldier Timothy Taylor, leaving him unfit to resume his old trade of seaman.[10]

After Wilderness, Grant slanted his army southeast toward the crossroads of Spotsylvania Courthouse. Killed along the way at Laurel Hill was James O'Neil of Sandwich. In three years' service, he had worked his way up from private to lieutenant. In attacking the base of the "muleshoe" salient at the May 12 Battle of Spotsylvania, the Fifty-eighth lost heavily. An exploding shell killed Captain Harley, an English "gentleman" who had come to this country over the wishes of his father and enlisted to fight in a foreign war. During nine months' service in the Forty-third, he had become friends with Charles Upham, and with enlistment up, Harley had come to Chatham with his companion and boarded at Eliza J. Smith's. Members of Harley's regiment, including Francis S. Cahoon of Chatham, buried him near the Harris House, a private residence used as a field hospital.[11]

Another Chatham soldier killed at Spotsylvania was Nathan Eldridge. Ebenezer Smalley thought he stood too long atop a parapet, making himself an easy target for a sharpshooter. Hyannis brick maker Ebenezer Eldridge was killed the same way. When Ezra B. Ryder saw Freeman Hall Jr. being led to the rear with a profusely bleeding gunshot wound to the head, he called out to his West Harwich neighbor but Hall did not respond;

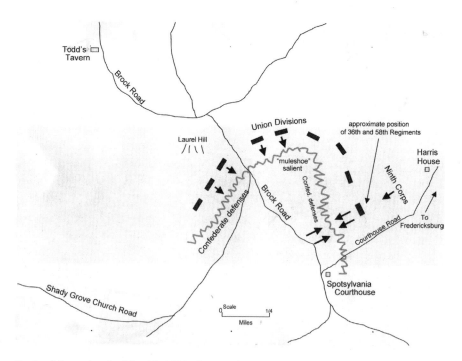

Battle of Spotsylvania, May 12, 1864. *Courtesy of the author.*

Right: James O'Neil, Sandwich, Ninth Regiment. *Courtesy U.S. Army Heritage and Education Center.*

Below: Charles M. Upham and William Harley, Chatham, Fifth-eighth Regiment. *Courtesy U.S. Army Heritage and Education Center.*

he soon died. Another fatality was James Ward of Sandwich, fighting in the Thirty-sixth Regiment and who was just ten days from completing a three-year enlistment and going home. Benjamin Wixon of Brewster died of wounds a day after the battle. Wounded were Ansel Studley, George S. Studley and David Ryder, who were later hospitalized together at three different facilities. Moses Doane was shot through the spine, and Zebina Dill of Chatham was captured.[12]

Hospitalized after Spotsylvania at Fredericksburg with gunshot wound of the arm and intestinal disease was Aaron Snow. Samuel Harding of Chatham obtained him medicine, changed his clothing and made him as comfortable as he could. Harding also wrote his wife, Hannah, telling her to tell Snow's wife, Rebecca, that he was looking after Aaron. The letter intentionally misled both wives that their husbands were better off than they truly were. "They needed no addition to their anxiety," wrote Harding.[13]

Telegraph operator William C. Hall tapped out dispatches to Washington and corps headquarters at Spotsylvania. Enemy shells frequently brought down lines, requiring operators to make the dangerous climb up poles to splice wires. When one operator did this, he would tell his cohorts, "If I stop a shell, send my things home." A dispatch from Grant at Spotsylvania to Washington contained one of the most famous lines of war: "I...propose to fight it out on this line if it takes all summer." Hall may have sent it.[14]

The Fortieth Regiment, in improved health because of thirty-three barrels of apples and other foodstuffs forwarded by Barnstable citizens, on May 6 reached Bermuda Hundred, Virginia, from South Carolina and joined General Butler's army. His orders were to advance toward Richmond to take pressure off Grant. The advance, however, was so slow it gave the enemy time to assemble a strong opposing force. On the morning of May 16, it counterattacked and mauled the Union at a sharp bend of the James River called Drewry's Bluff. Forced to flee from rifle pits, Edwin Bearse eluded a hailstorm of bullets. "Balls were everywhere, between my legs, arms, by my ears but still I kept on [running] expecting every moment was the last for me on Earth," he wrote in a May 17 letter to his sister. "Both of my companions and tent mates are gone, two of the best fellows in the Co." he continued, referring to William Gifford, shot through the jaw, and Cyrus Fish, captured. Also captured was William Dixon of Barnstable Village.[15]

Shot through the lungs in the Drewry's Bluff debacle was Solomon Otis, also of the village. He had joined the Fortieth at Beaufort, South Carolina, two months after his son Samuel had died and been buried there. Gunfire was too hot when Solomon was hit to allow comrades to reach him and hear his last words. Bearse, referring to his commanders and shot-up Company E, sighed, "The fact is the rebs out Generaled us and here we are what remains of us."[16]

After Spotsylvania, Grant angled south again. In fighting at the crossing of the North Anna River, George W. Childs of the Fifty-sixth was mortally wounded. At the crossroads battle of Cold Harbor, the Confederates employed to deadly effectiveness an art they had now mastered, creating defensive positions that maximized field of fire, leveling Union soldiers by scores as they came at them in frontal assaults. Struck down were Captain Charles Upham and his sergeant, Nathaniel B. Smith, who had left Amherst College to enlist and, at his death, carried a New Testament given to him by his fiancée. Others killed were Francis Armstrong, Benjamin Bassett and John Bolton of Chatham; Kelly Chase, Amos Ryder and Amos Wixon of Dennis; James Blagden of Barnstable; James P. Atkins of Yarmouth; and Jeremiah Bennett of Provincetown. The remains of the latter two lie with 2,008 other Union soldiers in the Cold Harbor National Cemetery, brought there for proper interment from improvised burials elsewhere on the battlefield.[17]

Shot through both legs at Cold Harbor was John B. Tuttle. Charles Mullett of Chatham helped carry him to the field hospital. After a night's stay, he went by army wagon to White House Landing and then on to Chestnut Hill Hospital in Philadelphia. After Mullett himself was wounded two weeks later, he and Tuttle shared a ward at Chestnut Hill.[18]

In mid-June, farmer Stephen Howes, who lived in Dennis Village "along the wagon road about 8 miles from Barnstable the county seat," received word that his son Stephen R. had been wounded at Spotsylvania; that he was in Armory Square Hospital in Washington; and that his case was "a very doubtful one." Howes left immediately for Washington, arrived in time to see his son and was hopeful of bringing him home but he took a turn for the worse and died June 23.[19]

Nathaniel B. Smith, Chatham, Fifty-eighth Regiment. *Courtesy U.S. Army Heritage and Education Center.*

The gravestones of James P. Atkins (left) and Jeremiah Bennett in Cold Harbor Cemetery. *Courtesy of the author.*

MISCELLANEOUS ACTIVITIES

Daniel M. Hall from the Bound Brook part of Wellfleet enlisted in the Second Massachusetts Cavalry in February 1864. Two months later, he wrote his father from his camp at Vienna, Virginia, describing his situation: "Well i have got my horse and armes. We carry a sabber [*sic*] and a pistol and a carbine…I look first rate." Two weeks later, his horse was gone: "I drew a big read horse but he was so awkward that the orderly sergeant gave him to another man and I have the first pick of the next lot that comes." He was on stable guard, meaning he had to feed and clean the horses and make sure none was taken out without orders.[20]

The Second Cavalry patrolled for guerilla bands that raided Union supply lines in Virginia, an activity Hall called "tip top fun," adding, "We privates confisscate from the farmers. I had as likes be hear as a fishing." His second horse, more coordinated than his first, could "jump a ditch or fence like a good fellow." Hall went on one too many patrols, however; during one on July 6, he was captured by Mosby's Rangers. A month later, he died in a South Carolina prisoner of war camp of gangrene of the foot.[21]

Hall wasn't the only Cape trooper vexed by guerillas. During General Banks's May retreat in the Louisiana Red River Expedition, James Ewer's Third Cavalry was attacked by Quantrill's Raiders at Snaggy Point, and Ewer was shot in the finger, a serious matter for bugler Ewer. The Third, with fifteen men of Provincetown and five from other parts of the Cape, departed Louisiana in July under orders for Virginia's Shenandoah Valley.

Left behind because of sickness was Henry Besse of Woods Hole. When his father Willard learned this, he asked neighbor Prince Robinson go to New Orleans to bring him home. Unfortunately, when Robinson got there, Henry was dead and buried; his body was not brought back.[22]

In February 1864, Giles M. Pease, an assistant surgeon in the black Fifty-fourth Regiment, went with it from South Carolina to Jacksonville. In preparation for its return to the Palmetto State, he placed his medical supplies of twenty-four bottles of spiritus frumenti (whiskey) and six of spirits vini gallici (brandy) on a steamer. Someone on board apparently needed a few doses of the "medicine" because when the steamer arrived, the packing crates were broken open and

James K. Ewer, Barnstable, Third Cavalry. *Courtesy U.S. Army Heritage and Education Center.*

the contents missing. In North Carolina, former Sandwich saloon keeper Obed M. Fish, a lieutenant of the Second Massachusetts Heavy Artillery, took an unsought trip south when Confederates seized the Union garrison at Plymouth, captured him and sent him to a prisoner of war camp in Georgia.[23]

PETERSBURG

On June 12, Grant's huge army quietly slipped out of the foul trenches at Cold Harbor, pulled back and, in one of the great troop movements of the war, crossed the James on a 2,100-foot pontoon bridge. For once in the campaign begun in May, Grant was a step ahead of his adversary, Lee. While awaiting crossing, Everett Doane of Harwichport summarized the condition of his Fifty-eighth Regiment in a letter to his mother: "When we left Readville We had seven hundred [men] and now we hant got but two hundred left. Our regment has been badly cut up."[24]

Once across the river, Grant moved against the important—and stoutly fortified—railroad hub of Petersburg. Trying to prevent a siege and keep ahead of Lee, he ordered attacks on the city's defenses. In one on June 16, Thomas Jones of Marstons Mills and the Twenty-fourth Regiment was shot in the abdomen. He and Noah Bradford—who still was not over his South Carolina ailments—traveled together by boat to a hospital at Fortress Monroe. On June 17, Jesse Pendergrast of Truro and the Twenty-fourth was struck by a piece of shell that carried away his left arm and part of his right hand. Ebenezer Smalley, who had enlisted to join the mass of soldiery trying to shove the Confederate "boulder" off the cliff, sustained mortal wounds on June 18. Five days later, a sharpshooter killed Lieutenant Franklin Hammond of Chatham. Samuel Harding was at the James River when the body arrived from Petersburg. "Our cousin Franklin has ended his duty on earth," he wrote Hannah. The cost of embalming, encasing and transporting the body home, which reached Chatham on August 3, totaled $108.00.[25]

Jesse Pendergrast, Truro, circa 1880. *Courtesy National Archives.*

Grant's efforts were for naught. The two armies settled into a grim and protracted siege at Petersburg. Writing from there on Independence Day—the fourth of the war—Edwin Nickerson of North Chatham and the Fifty-eighth reported, "A high old 4th it is. I have been firing at the rebs untill I have got tired." Although he had provided support for his family when a civilian, he could provide none as a soldier because all Company A officers had been killed and company books lost. Indeed, he wanted his family to send him money so he could buy a little tobacco and some food from the sutler. "I am almost tired of living on hard bread and fresh beef and coffee." Faring better than Nickerson at Petersburg were the flies. They are "as big as my fist. if they don't eat me up I shall bee glad."[26]

Later in July, a canal boat carrying officers' baggage, medical stores, regimental books and band music of the Fifty-sixth Regiment sank in the James. This was especially serious for Rawlins Atkins, now regimental quartermaster. He, the bandmaster and a detail of Atkins's men went to the site and salvaged what they could, spending much time in water up to their waists.[27]

Within Burnside's Corps and the Fifty-eighth's brigade was the Forty-eighth Pennsylvania—no ordinary regiment. Many of its men were coal miners. Its commander, a mining engineer, conceived of tunneling under the

Franklin Hammond, Chatham, Fifty-eighth Regiment. *Courtesy U.S. Army Heritage and Education Center.*

Confederate lines and blowing a breech in them with a massive powder detonation. Tunneling progressed through July, and by the end of the month, it was ready. For the plan to succeed, the explosion would have to be followed up with a rapid, well-coordinated infantry assault. Burnside chose his division of black troops to lead it because they were less worn-down than his three white divisions. The plan, however, was overruled at the last moment over concern that if the assault failed, it would look as if the Union army high command was willing to sacrifice black soldiers as "cannon fodder."

At the eleventh hour, Burnside had to find a new lead division. When none of his three white division commanders volunteered, he had them draw straws. General James Ledlie, said to have a drinking problem, "won" the honor. One of his regiments was the Fifty-sixth. After the explosion, which hurled earth and flame fifty feet into the air and created a huge crater, the assault forces encountered delay in climbing over their own parapets and negotiating obstructions between the lines, all the time choking on fumes and dust. Delay translated into lost momentum and breakdown of order. "It was perfect pandemonium," reported Colonel Weld.[28]

The Battle of the Crater, as it was later called, gained nothing for the Union. The Fifty-eighth, which followed the Fifty-sixth into the chasm, suffered terribly. It began the day with two hundred officers and men and finished with only twenty-eight. Eighty-three from the regiment were captured or missing, eight from Harwich alone. Pliny Freeman of Chatham, who had enlisted after completing a voyage to Lisbon on the bark *Schamyl*

Substitute form or contract for Nehemiah P. Baker, Falmouth. *Courtesy National Archives.*

under Captain Levi Taylor, was wounded by being thrown into a protruding log by an exploding shell. Everett Doane, who was captured and then taken back, wrote, "We should have taken Peatersburg if it had not been for the oficers. They was all drunk and we was defeated dreadfully. If it had not been for rum we should have been in Peatersburg."[29]

The Fifty-sixth sustained fifty casualties. Taken prisoner was Elkanah Smith of Provincetown. He had moved there from Eastham in 1861 and served as mate of the fresh-fishing schooner *Black Swan*. As principal support of indigent parents in Eastham, he furnished them $3.00 per month from his wages. Paroled from prison on October 15 and admitted to a hospital in Annapolis on the 17th, he died on the 26th. Also captured was Taylor Small Jr., who had had the whiskey-drinking dust-up with John E. Smith. Mortally wounded from the black division that eventually entered the fray was John Romeo, a substitute for Hugh G. Donaldson of Falmouth.[30]

Letters from Petersburg

The siege went on. It was a dreary, dirty, disease-ridden existence. Life for Edwin Nickerson was one of two days on picket duty, followed by two in the rear. "Our picket lines is about 50 or 60 yards apart. We lay out here 48 hours and get roasted then back in the woods for 48 hours," he wrote. Sidney Brooks of Harwich visited the front at Petersburg in August as a delegate of the U.S. Christian Commission. His first view of it, gained after climbing stairs up the Appomattox River bank, was one he would never forget: "A suffocating heat and the air filled with clouds of dust, the desert-like appearance of every foot of ground, the thousands of tents…the blinding dust raised by the trains of mules and horses and galloping of cavalry which we had to avoid as we do a driving snowstorm."[31]

Simeon C. Childs Jr. wrote home in August inquiring about his cousin Job, also in the Fourteenth Battery. He had not been heard from since June when he had gone two miles behind the lines to Ninth Corps Hospital. In a September 14 letter, Simeon reported that the Fourteenth was in the artillery reserve and for good reason—not enough horses or men. "Our rations are getting worse than ever," he wrote. "Bare hard tack and coffee." Three days later, he developed severe intestinal disease, necessitating comrade Charles Holmes to write home for him. Strong enough on September 24 to resume writing home, his thoughts again went to his missing cousin. "Have you heard from Job. I dream of him every night almost." Simeon died of

Sidney Brooks, Harwich, in Christian Commission uniform. *Courtesy Harwich Historical Society.*

disease nine days later. Just what happened to Job is unclear.[32]

Also in the Petersburg trenches was the Fortieth Regiment. When one of its privates, Samuel Wood of North Sandwich, was hospitalized, comrade Henry B. Baker carried gruel daily two miles to him at Ninth Corps Hospital. Wood was a member of the Herring Pond tribe of the Wampanaog, Baker was a Cape Cod Railroad section master. Baker's efforts were in vain, however, because Wood died. "He [has] bin a brother to me," wrote a grief-stricken Baker in a letter to Wood's wife and family. "He was all the life to the Regt."[33]

TRIBULATION UP NORTH

One of the Southern commerce raiders that superseded the privateers was the *Tallahassee*, which raided Northern shipping lanes in the summer of 1864. As the cod-fishing schooner *Mercy A. Howes* of Chatham, with Samuel Howes as sailing master, was returning from the Grand Banks on August 15, just three days' sail from home, the raider captured and burned her. Howes and his wife, Elizabeth, had already had enough misfortune for one year, losing their son Seth at the Wilderness in May. This, then, the loss of a full fare of fish from a whole summer's work, was more than backbreaking. The luckless Howes was landed by his captor at Yarmouth, Nova Scotia, and from there, he made it home through the assistance of the American consul.[34]

Others had bad luck. Sergeant Benjamin H. Matthews of Yarmouthport, who came through three years' campaigning with the Fortieth Regiment relatively unscathed, met with an accident on the final leg of his trip home. He was part of a detachment of convalescent soldiers that on October 15 left a hospital at New Haven, Connecticut, for Massachusetts. Not far along, their train derailed and slammed into rocks, killing and injuring many, and breaking Matthews's leg. After good service in the Thirty-ninth Regiment, Benjamin Batchelder entered the Veterans Reserve Corps and was detailed to assist at the conscript camp at Fairhaven, Connecticut, in November. While there, a gun fell from a rack, discharged and shot him.[35]

Ansel L. Studley passed through hospitals in Fredericksburg, Virginia, Washington and New Haven, Connecticut, after suffering a shell wound, and around October 15, he arrived home in South Dennis. Upon learning this, neighbors Sally Cahoon and Eliza A. Pierce called on him, found him very sick and were with him when he died ten days later. The young man was probably no older than seventeen. Back in December 1863, his mother Polly had scrawled her "x" on consent papers for his underage enlistment.[36]

PRISONS AND PEACE

The majority of captured Cape soldiers were incarcerated at Andersonville, Georgia; Danville, Virginia; and Salisbury, North Carolina. Men captured in the period of March–June 1864 went to Andersonville. Of fifteen Cape men imprisoned there, only three survived: Thomas B. Bourne of Monument, Howard H.P. Lovell of Sandwich and William Dixon. Had those three not escaped or been transferred, they too might have died. Captives often had an intermediate stop in Richmond. Zebina Dill of Chatham spent three weeks there before leaving on May 31 for Andersonville. One of the more remarkable Cape-related Civil War documents is a letter sent home from Richmond by Francis L. Doane on July 5 five weeks after he, his brother Solomon and North Harwich neighbor Moses Handy were captured at North Anna, Virginia. All would die within three months at Andersonville. Eight Cape soldiers have marked graves there.[37]

Men captured at the Crater went to Danville. Of 15 Cape men taken there, 6 died. Salisbury was an abandoned cotton factory. Almost all Cape soldiers imprisoned there were captured at the September 30 Petersburg battle of Peebles Farm or October 19 Shenandoah Valley battle of Cedar Creek. Of 15 Cape men incarcerated there, only George W. Swift of

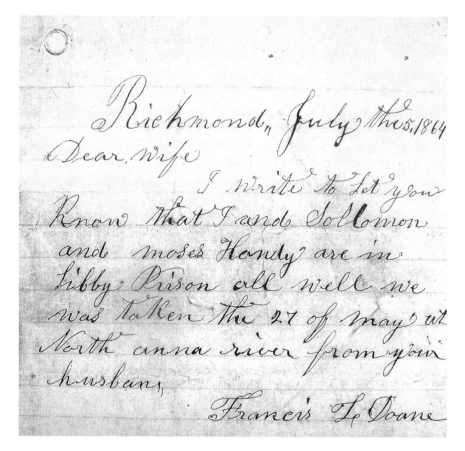

A letter sent home by Francis L. Doane from prison. *Courtesy National Archives.*

Falmouth and Henry Mallows of Chatham survived. Salisbury's population peaked at 8,700 men in early November with the arrival of Swift, Barnabas Cook, Shubael Linnell, James McKowen and other Cedar Creek captives. Ezra B. Ryder escaped while being transferred from Richmond to Salisbury and made it back to Harwich but never recovered from prison-induced scurvy; he died in 1876.[38]

On February 19, 1865, a prisoner exchange was worked out at Salisbury. Sicker men such as Barnabas G. Baker of Brewster went by train to Richmond while stronger ones such as Swift and Bourne traveled by foot and train to Wilmington, North Carolina, arriving around March 2. As good fortune would have it, the transport *Tillie* under Captain Henry Bourne, brother of Thomas, and crewman Freeman Hatch of Waquoit, friend of Swift, was at Wilmington. Both just-released men came aboard, more dead than alive. (Thomas had to be carried.) Both suffered mental impairment from their privations—Swift had trouble remembering he was from Cape Cod—but they made full recoveries.[39]

Coming north through South Carolina was General Sherman's army, and in it the Massachusetts Thirty-third. Nathan Gill, now a sergeant and veteran of three years' hard service, was part of a foraging party of an army living off the land. "Brought in 400 wate of Bacon and plenty of poultry and a splendid horse," he wrote February 5 after scouring the environs of Robertville, South Carolina. A few days later, he assisted in destroying tracks of the Augusta and Charleston Railroad.[40]

Thomas B. Bourne, Sandwich, Fifty-eighth Regiment. *Courtesy U.S. Army Heritage and Education Center.*

On April 2, 1865, General Lee and his starving army evacuated the trenches at Petersburg and plodded west. Part of the closely pursuing Union army was the Fifty-eighth—that is, what was left of it. A lame and "used up" David P. Ryder used his gun for a crutch when he couldn't find a stick. Lee surrendered April 9 at Appomattox. Harwich millwright William Field, who had gone out with the Thirty-ninth Regiment three years earlier, witnessed the event and even brought home a souvenir—a piece of limb of an apple tree in the yard of the surrender site.[41]

After four years, peace returned. The *Patriot* reported the news in its April 11 edition. In every town and village of the Cape, bells rang and cannons roared. "Our citizens are everywhere exultant," reported Phinney. Cape Cod's tattered companies straggled home. David Kendrick of Chatham furnished the *Patriot* with the long list of casualties of Company A of the

Fifty-eighth. July saw the arrival of Company H of the Thirty-eighth, the Falmouth Company. Seven of its original twenty-eight members were dead; ten others had come home early on disability discharges. Thomas Gibbs and Charles Little of Pocasset, who had lied about their ages to enlist, were stationed in Washington after the war ended. After Thomas entered a hospital, Little wrote Thomas's mother, Ann Maria Gibbs, on June 28: "Miss Gibbs don't you worry about him…you may look for me [and] Thomas 18 of Juli." Seven days later, Thomas died. The sacrifices of Gibbs and the Cape companies had not been in vain. Through the efforts of them, other soldiers, civilians of the Cape and the rest of the North, Ebenezer Smalley's "great boulder" had been pushed off the cliff. The Confederacy had been destroyed, and the Union was restored.[42]

Peace brought no end of the war for Cape Cod's numerous ship captains, owners and crewmen victimized in captures at sea by the CSS *Alabama* and other Confederate commerce raiders. For these unfortunates, the Cape's Civil War era continued, a story too long for the scope of this book. Only with the final Alabama Claims awards in the mid-1880s, often to heirs of victims, did the Cape's long chapter of the Civil War finally close.

CHAPTER 8

FINAL TRUMPET

Scattered about Cape Cod are gravestones, plaques and monuments to soldiers, sailors and civilians of Barnstable County who gave their lives to Civil War causes. Other war participants, however, who made that same sacrifice have nothing—on the Cape or elsewhere—to mark their presence in this world and passage out of it. Perhaps the best way to remember all is to discuss a few, in a brief cemetery tour, starting in Barnstable and ending in Provincetown.

(1) Eliza A. Chamberlain: Buried in her family's plot in Lothrop Hill Cemetery in Barnstable Village is Chamberlain, perhaps the Cape's most prominent woman of the war. Born in 1837 in Barnstable Village to Captain Joshua and Betsey Loring Chamberlain, she was a student in 1850 at the Barnstable Academy and, around 1860, a schoolteacher in Osterville. During the first years of the war, she was secretary of the Barnstable Village Ladies Relief Society, while, in early 1864, she collected sixty-five dollars for the Boston Young Men's Christian Commission. In August, she and Mrs. Joseph (Elizabeth) Day made blackberry cordials for the soldiers.[1]

Chamberlain moved to Washington in the fall of 1864 and began teaching at the Mount Zion Freedman's School for liberated slaves in Georgetown, sponsored by the Pennsylvania Freedman's Relief Association and where A.E. Newton was superintendent. She lived in his residence in Washington. When not teaching, she ministered to sick soldiers at Soldiers Rest, eight miles away in Alexandria, Virginia. Her school—a "dark, damp and ill-ventilated" room in the basement of Mount Zion Church—supposedly infected her with tuberculosis.[2]

When Washington's freedman's schools became graded in 1867, Chamberlain became head of the grammar department and principal of

Eliza A. Chamberlain's grave in Lothrop Hill Cemetery in Barnstable Village. *Courtesy Cynthia Moore, Cape Cod.*

several schools. She had fifty pupils of all ages and sizes in her classroom. As a teacher of blacks, she endured the taunts of whites of the neighborhood. Weakened and close to death from her disease in 1870, she forced herself to travel from Washington to Barnstable Village, as she felt it wrong to make her frail mother come to her. Chamberlain died there on June 20, 1870. Buried with her is her brother Allen, who died in September 1865, also in Barnstable Village, after having served on transports during the war.[3]

(2) Simeon Cahoon: In East Harwich's Methodist Cemetery is the simple yet attractive stone of Cahoon, born in 1843 and one of seven children of fisherman Stephen and Elizabeth Cahoon of that place. Simeon went to work young, going to sea in the 1850s on seasonal fishing voyages to the Grand Banks under neighbor and schooner captain George W. Nickerson, who applied the young man's earnings to the upkeep of the large family. In 1859, Cahoon shipped under Ensign Jerauld of Harwich for a voyage to the Grand Banks in the schooner *David Howes* of Chatham. His family used part of his wages from that voyage to buy two barrels of flour ($9.50 per barrel). A year later, he made a second voyage with Jerauld except in a different schooner.

Neighbor Danforth Steele was appointed guardian in 1862 of Stephen Cahoon, who had developed mental disease.[4]

Since Cahoon's family was too poor to own a house, Nickerson used Simeon's bounty money from his 1864 enlistment in the Fifty-eighth Regiment to buy an old house and move it to East Harwich for their use. Simeon was wounded in the arm at the Battle of the Wilderness and died on July 10, 1864, from amputation surgery at Washington's Armory Square Hospital. Without its principal breadwinner, the family had to rely on charity of friends and the town of Harwich to get by financially.[5]

Simeon Cahoon's grave in East Harwich Methodist Cemetery. *Courtesy Cynthia Moore, Cape Cod.*

(3) John L.D. Hopkins: Standing prominently in Truro's Congregational Churchyard Cemetery is an obelisk to Hopkins, born in 1843 to Isaac and Ruth Dyer Hopkins. His family's homestead was along the south side of the Pamet River. In the early 1860s, father and son worked on mackerel schooners that voyaged seasonally to the Bay of Chaleur, Gulf of St. Lawrence, Canada. Illness forced Isaac Hopkins to take up a less physically demanding trade, shoemaking, in 1863. Around 1864, his property consisted of a shoe shop, barn, half a dwelling house, brush land and a cow. His son John, like Simeon Cahoon, enlisted in the Fifty-eighth Regiment and, in early 1864, went off to war.[6]

"I pray that if it is gods will…we shall all meet around the fireside at home once more," wrote Hopkins on September 9, 1864, from Petersburg, Virginia. His modest wish was not to be; he was one of ten Cape soldiers captured twenty-one days later at Peebles Farm, Virginia, and taken to the Salisbury, North Carolina prison where he died on February 12, 1865, just a week before the prisoner exchange began. "With resignation and hope, he committed

John L.D. Hopkins's grave in Truro Congregational Church Cemetery. *Courtesy Cynthia Moore, Cape Cod.*

himself to God, who hears the sighing of the prisoner," reads the final line of the inscription on his monument.[7]

(4) George E. Crocker: Emblazoned with cannons, rifles and swords is the Provincetown Civil War monument, the most ornate of any on the Cape. Carved into one of its faces are names of Provincetowners who died in the war. One is George E. Crocker, who was born in West Barnstable in 1835. He moved to Provincetown around 1858 after marrying Josephine Smith of Orleans. In 1860, he was working in Provincetown as a dentist. A child was born to the Crockers that year.[8]

Crocker was a member of the Sandwich company that sailed to Fortress Monroe, Virginia, in May 1861. He apparently had musical as well as dental talents, because on January 30, 1862, he was promoted from musician of his company to fife major of the Twenty-ninth Regiment, to which the Sandwich company had been attached. A fife major had command of all ten fifers of a regiment (one per company, ten companies in a regiment). The tones of fifes announced, accompanied and ended many of the activities of camp. From the Cape came a dozen Civil War musicians—fifers, drummers and buglers—of whom Crocker seems to have been most prominent.[9]

Crocker came down with an intestinal illness in mid-1862, and around November, he received a medical discharge. Although Dr. Jeremiah Stone of Provincetown attended him, his condition was too severe to respond to medical care, and he died February 14, 1863.

CAPE COD CIVIL WAR TRANSPORT PERSONNEL

Name	Town	Vessel	Position	Years
1. Allen, Joshua D.	Harwich	schooner *Kate Field*	captain	1864
2. Arey, Elbridge G.	Wellfleet	steamer *Thames*	captain	1862–1865
3. Atkins, Joshua Jr.	Chatham	steamer *S.R. Spaulding*	mate, captain	1861–1865
4. Atwood, Eleazer H.	Wellfleet	schooner *Mary Standish*	captain	1862
5. Bacon, George W.	Barnstable	steamer *Rockland*	captain	1863–1864
6. Bacon, Nathaniel	Barnstable	steamer *Ranger*	captain	1864
7. Bacon, Nathaniel Jr.	Barnstable	steamer *Ranger*	captain	1865
8. Baker, Horatio N.	Barnstable	schooner *Howard*	captain	1863
9. Baker, John P.	Barnstable	schooner *Forest City*	crewman	1863
10. Baker, Oliver K.	Dennis	schooner *Avon*	captain	1864
11. Baxter, Edwin	Barnstable	brig *Benjamin Delano*	captain	1862–1863
12. Baxter, John	Dennis	steamer *Pocahontas*	captain	1863–1864
13. Baxter, Rodney	Barnstable	steamers *Mississippi, Clinton*	captain	1862–1863

Name	Town	Vessel	Position	Years
14. Baxter, Samuel	Dennis	steamer *Pocahontas*	mate	1863–1864
15. Baxter, Samuel S.	Barnstable	steamer *Empire City*	captain	1861–1865
16. Bearse, Harrison	Barnstable	schooner *Howard*	mate	1863
17. Bearse, Isaac M.	Chatham	bark *Guiding Star*	captain	1861–1863
18. Bearse, Owen	Barnstable	schooner *Charmer*	owner-agent	1862
19. Bearse, Prince	Barnstable	schooner *Village Gem*	captain	1862
20. Bearse, Wellington	Harwich	schooner *M.C. Durfee*	captain	1862
21. Berry, Horace N.	Harwich	brig *Mystic*	captain	1863–1865
22. Bourne, Henry A.	Sandwich	steamer *Tillie*	captain	1865
23. Brown, Thomas	Barnstable	schooner *Howard*	crewman	1863
24. Burgess, Freeman	Harwich	schooner *Elizabeth B.*	captain	1864
25. Burgess, James F.	Brewster	steamers *Guide*, *Ranger*	mate	1863–1864
26. Burgess, Stephen	Harwich	brig *Julia Ford*	mate	1862
27. Burlingame, Pardon	Barnstable	schooner *Charmer*	captain	1862
28. Cahoon, George W.	Barnstable	schooner *Forest City*	crewman	1863
29. Chamberlain, Allen	Barnstable	steamer *John Warner*	mate	1864
30. Clark, Elisha Jr.	Harwich	schooner *O.M. Pettit*	captain	1864
31. Crowell, Allen	Barnstable	schooner *Hattie Baker*	captain	1865
32. Crowell, Ebenezer	Yarmouth	steamer *John Warner*	mate	1864
33. Crowell, Ephraim	Barnstable	schooner *Herbert Manton*	captain	1862

Name	Town	Vessel	Position	Years
34. Crowell, Freeman III	Dennis	brig *John Freeman*	captain	1862
35. Crowell, George	Dennis	schooner *John Ponder*	captain	1864
36. Crowell, George W.	Dennis	schooner *Western Star*	captain	1864–1865
37. Crowell, Guilford	Dennis	schooner *Star*	captain	1862
		schooner *John Ponder Jr.*		1864
38. Crowell, Hersey	Dennis	schooner *Roxbury*	captain	1862
39. Crowell, Higgins	Yarmouth	steamer *Exact*	captain	1863-64
40. Crowell, John	Chatham	ship *Ocean Pearl*	captain	1862
41. Crowell, Luther	Dennis	schooner *La Plata*	captain	1865
42. Crowell, Pliny	Dennis	schooner *West Dennis*	captain	1863
43. Crowell, Sidney	Barnstable	steamer *Chesapeake*	captain	1861
44. Doane, Abiathur	Harwich	schooner *J.W. Allen*	mate	1863
45. Doane, Edwin F.	Harwich	schooner *J.W. Allen*	mate	1863
		steamer *C.W. Thomas*	captain	1864
46. Doane, Elbridge Jr.	Harwich	schooner *J.W. Allen*	captain	1863
47. Eldridge, John	Yarmouth	steamers *Atlantic*, *Baltic* and *Fulton*	captain	1862–1863
48. Eldridge, Joseph	Dennis	schooner *Westover*	captain	1865
49. Eldridge, Oliver	Yarmouth	steamers *State of Maine*, *Atlantic* and *Baltic*	captain	1861–1864
50. Eldridge, Seth N.	Chatham	schooner *Virginia Price*	captain	1862–1863
51. Eldridge, Ward	Falmouth	steamer *City of New York*	mate	1862
52. Evans, William	Dennis	steamer *John Adams*	captain	1864

Name	Town	Vessel	Position	Years
53. Fisk, Luther	Dennis	schooner *Sarah M. Smith*	captain	1862
54. Fuller, Edwin	Barnstable	schooner *Susan M. Tyler*	captain	1865
55. Gould, David Jr.	Chatham	bark *Horace Scudder*	captain	1865
56. Gorham, Oliver	Yarmouth	bark *Paramount*	captain	1863
57. Hall, Gideon	Dennis	schooner *John Farnum*	captain	1862
58. Hallett, Benjamin	Barnstable	schooner *Louisa*	captain	1862
59. Hallett, Charles	Barnstable	brig *Randolph*	captain	1862
60. Hallett, William A.	Barnstable	steamer *Ben Deford*	captain	1861–1864
61. Hallett, William W.	Barnstable	schooner *Forest City*	mate	1863
62. Hamblen, Lloyd B.	Barnstable	bark *Guerilla*	captain	1862
63. Harding, Archeleus	Chatham	bark *Chief*	captain	1865
64. Harding, David J.	Chatham	ship *Windermere*	captain	1862–1863
65. Harding, Isaiah S.	Dennis	steamer *Dudley Buck*	captain	1863–1864
66. Harding, Joseph	Chatham	schooner *Julia Anna*	agent	1862–1863
67. Harding, Samuel S.	Chatham	bark *Young Turk*	captain	1862
68. Hatch, Freeman S.	Falmouth	steamer *Tillie*	crewman	1863
69. Howes, Daniel W.	Dennis	steamer *John Rice*	captain	1864–1865
70. Howes, Elisha	Barnstable	steamer *Star of the West*	captain	1861
71. Howes, Francis M.	Chatham	steamer *S.R. Spaulding*	mate	1861
72. Howes, Solomon	Chatham	steamer *S.R. Spaulding*	captain	1861–1864
73. Howes, Thomas P.	Dennis	ship *Black Prince*	captain	1861–1862
74. Jaggar, Cyrus B.	Barnstable	schooner *Forest City*	crewman	1863

Cape Cod Civil War Transport Personnel

Name	Town	Vessel	Position	Years
75. Kelley, David N.	Barnstable	bark *Island City*	captain	1861–1862
		schooner *Abbie Bursley*		1865
76. Kelley, Fernandus	Dennis	schooner *Mountain Avenue*	captain	1862
77. Lawrence, Samuel	Falmouth	steamer *Tillie*	mate	1864–1865
78. Lewis, Enoch	Barnstable	schooner *Louis Spanier*	captain	1862
79. Lewis, Thomas C.	Falmouth	tug *Thomas Foulkes*	captain	1864
80. Lincoln, Edgar	Brewster	steamer *City of Bath*	captain	1864
81. Lombard, Ebbren A.	Truro	schooner *Etta G. Fogg*	captain	1862
82. Loring, George	Barnstable	steamer *Henry Morrison*	captain	1861–1865
83. Loring, George H.	Yarmouth	brig *Elisha Doane*	captain	1862
84. Loveland, Winslow	Chatham	steamer *Joseph Whitney*	captain	1861
85. Lovell, Russell	Barnstable	schooner *Forest City*	captain	1863
86. Matthews, Atkins	Yarmouth	schooner *Howard*	crewman	1863
87. Matthews, Seleck	Yarmouth	steamer *Cambridge*	captain	1861
88. Mayo, David E.	Chatham	bark *Amazonian*	captain/owner	1862–1863
89. Mayo, Sewell S.	Truro	schooner *J. Paine*	captain	1864
90. Nickerson, Allen	Yarmouth	schooner *Fannie Currie*	captain	1863
91. Nickerson, Asa W.	Dennis	schooner *A.H. Manchester*	captain	1862
92. Nickerson, Cyrus	Dennis	schooner *E. Nickerson*	captain	1862
93. Nickerson, Moses	Chatham	bark *Mary Edson*	captain	1862

113

Name	Town	Vessel	Position	Years
94. Nye, Joseph W.	Falmouth	steamer *Potomska*	captain	1861
		steamer *City of New York*		1862
95. Orlando, John	Yarmouth	schooner *Julia Smith*	captain	1863
96. Paine, Isaac	Wellfleet	schooner *George S. Fogg*	captain	1862
97. Paine, Thomas	Wellfleet	schooner *S.A. Hammond*	captain	1865
98. Parker, D.P.W.	Barnstable	steamer *Mississippi*	mate	1862
99. Parker, F.A.	Barnstable	schooner *Owen Bearse*	captain	1865
100. Payne, John A.	Chatham	brig *Julia Ford*	captain	1862
101. Peterson, Isaac	Dennis	schooner *Rhodella Blew*	captain	1863–1864
102. Purvere, Washington	Wellfleet	steamer *Ranger*	crewman	1863
103. Rich, Lyman B.	Wellfleet	schooner *E.M. Dyer*	captain	1864
104. Ryder, Richard	Chatham	bark *Daniel Webster*	captain	1862
		schooner *Manhasset*		1863–1864
105. Sears, Benjamin P.	Dennis	schooner *Searsville*	captain	1862
106. Sears, Edward Jr.	Dennis	schooner *Victor*	captain	1862
107. Sears, Elisha F.	Brewster	propeller *City of Bath*	captain	1863–1864
108. Sears, Winthrop	Yarmouth	ship *Conquest*	captain	1862
109. Smith, Enoch	Chatham	schooner *R.G. Porter*	captain	1862
110. Snow, Josiah Jr.	Orleans	ship *Idaho*	co-owner	1862
111. Snow, Sylvanus A.	Barnstable	schooner *Alida*	captain	1862
112. Sparrow, Thomas	Chatham	bark *Wild Gazelle*	captain	1862

Cape Cod Civil War Transport Personnel

Name	Town	Vessel	Position	Years
113. Steele, Ephraim P.	Chatham	schooner *Millard Fillmore*	captain	1862
114. Waitt, Joseph	Barnstable	schooner *Forest City*	crewman	1863
115. Young, Franklin	Barnstable	steamer *Empire City*	mate	1861

CAPE COD
CIVIL WAR OFFICERS

Name	Town	Last Unit	Highest Rank
1. Atherton, James H.	Sandwich	4th MA Heavy Art	first lieutenant
2. Atkins, Rawlins T.	Provincetown	56th MA Regiment	first lieutenant
3. Baker, Charles G.	Barnstable	1st NY Marine Art	captain
4. Baker, Ezra C.	Barnstable	28th MA Regiment	second lieutenant
5. Baker, Scotto B.N.	Harwich	58th MA Regiment	first lieutenant
6. Baxter, Benjamin D.	Barnstable	1st NY Marine Art	second lieutenant
7. Blossom, Henry C.	Barnstable	40th MA Regiment	first lieutenant
8. Bourne, Joshua W.	Sandwich	7th MO Regiment	captain
9. Brady, Charles	Sandwich	29th MA Regiment	captain
10. Chase, Heman Jr.	Harwich	58th MA Regiment	second lieutenant
11. Chipman, Charles	Sandwich	29th MA Regiment	major
12. Cobb, Alfred S.	Brewster	1st Reg. CO Vols.	first lieutenant
13. Collins, John T.	Sandwich	1st Hvy. U.S. Col'd	lieutenant colonel
14. Day, Joseph M.	Barnstable	40th MA Regiment	major
15. Doane, Henry	Orleans	43rd MA Regiment	captain
16. Dudley, Albion M.	Provincetown	58th MA Regiment	captain

Name	Town	Last Unit	Highest Rank
17. Ellington, Raymond	Provincetown	3rd MA Cavalry	first lieutenant
18. Fish, Obed M.	Sandwich	2nd MA Heav. Art	captain
19. Freeman, Hartwell	Sandwich	81st U.S. Colored	first lieutenant
20. French, Edward B.	Chatham	39th MA Regiment	chaplain
21. Hallett, Joseph L.	Barnstable	31st MA Regiment	first lieutenant
22. Hamblin, Joseph E.	Yarmouth	65th NY Regiment	brigadier major general
23. Hammond, Frank. D.	Chatham	58th MA Regiment	second lieutenant
24. Harley, William H.	Chatham	58th MA Regiment	captain
25. Harper, William H.	Sandwich	40th MA Regiment	captain
26. Higgins, Benjamin L.	Brewster	86th NY Regiment	colonel
27. Holmes, James M.	Provincetown	159th NY Regiment	first lieutenant
28. Hopkins, Edward F.	Brewster	7th MA Regiment	captain
29. Howland, James H.	Barnstable	40th MA Regiment	second lieutenant
30. Hughes, Hezekiah P.	Truro	3rd MA Cavalry	second lieutenant
31. Jones, Asa S.	Harwich	6th U.S. Colored	second lieutenant
32. Kern, Henry A.	Sandwich	29th MA Regiment	first lieutenant
33. Knowles, Alfred H.	Orleans	54th MA Regiment	first lieutenant
34. Landers, John B.	Falmouth	5th RI Heavy Art	first lieutenant
35. Lewis, Eugene	Harwich	1st NY Cavalry	first lieutenant
36. Lewis, Frederick T.	Falmouth	97th IL Regiment	captain
37. Lewis, Horatio F.	Chatham	58th MA Regiment	second lieutenant
38. Lewis, James M.	Falmouth	28th WI Regiment	colonel
39. Lombard, Richard T.	Truro	11th MA Regiment	major
40. Madigan, Joseph J.	Sandwich	29th MA Regiment	first lieutenant
41. Munsell, George N.	Harwich	35th MA Regiment	assistant surgeon

Cape Cod Civil War Officers

Name	Town	Last Unit	Highest Rank
42. Myrick, George	Yarmouth	5th MA Regiment	first lieutenant
43. Nickerson, George H.	Orleans	43rd MA Regiment	second lieutenant
44. Nye, Ephraim B.	Sandwich	14th MA Artillery	second lieutenant
45. O'Neil, James	Sandwich	9th MA Regiment	second lieutenant
46. Paine, Amasa E.	Truro	104th U.S. Colored	surgeon
47. Paine, Joseph W.	Wellfleet	2nd MA Heavy Art	captain
48. Pease, Giles M.	Sandwich	54th MA Regiment	assistant surgeon
49. Pineo, Peter	Barnstable	U.S. Vols, med dept	lieutenant colonel
50. Rider, Godfrey Jr.	Provincetown	33rd MA Regiment	lieutenant colonel
51. Shiverick, Andrew F.	Falmouth	28th WI Regiment	captain
52. Small, John F.	Provincetown	19th MA Regiment	first lieutenant
53. Swift, Elijah	Falmouth	38th MA Regiment	first lieutenant
54. Swift, John L.	Falmouth	3rd MA Cavalry	captain
55. Underwood, Benjamin W.	Harwich	72nd IL Regiment	first lieutenant
56. Underwood, Nathan	Harwich	72nd IL Regiment	first lieutenant
57. Upham, Charles M.	Chatham	58th MA Regiment	captain

APPENDIX C

CAPE COD CIVIL WAR DEATHS

Key: Soldiers and Marines Killed in Action (kia), Died of Wounds (dow) or Died of Disease (dod)

Name	Town	Unit	Circumstances
1. Alton, Samuel T.	Sandwich	2nd MA Reg't	dow, Gettysburg, July 17, 1863
2. Armstrong, Francis	Chatham	58th MA Reg't	dow, Cold Harbor, July 17, 1864
3. Atkins, James P.	Yarmouth	58th MA Reg't	kia, Cold Harbor, VA, June 8, 1864
4. Avery, Watson D.	Sandwich	40th MA Reg't	dod, Miners Hill, VA, Oct. 27, 1862
5. Baker, Barnabas G.	Brewster	58th MA Reg't	dod Baltimore, MD, April 11, 1865
6. Baker, James H.	Falmouth	38th MA Reg't	dod East Falmouth Nov. 27, 1863
7. Baker, Winslow	Harwich	58th MA Reg't	dod, Salisbury, NC, prison, Dec. 31, 1864
8. Bassett, Benjamin F.	Chatham	58th MA Reg't	dow, Cold Harbor, June 23, 1864
9. Bassett, Clarence	Barnstable	45th MA Reg't	kia, Kinston, NC, Dec. 14, 1862

Name	Town	Unit	Circumstances
10. Bassett, William H.H.	Harwich	58th MA Reg't	dod, Danville, VA, prison, Jan. 16, 1865
11. Baxter, Alpheus E.	Dennis	9th IL Cavalry	dod, Dennis, June 19, 1864
12. Bearse, George H.	Barnstable	45th MA Reg't	dod, New Bern, NC, Jan. 7, 1863
13. Bennett, Jeremiah	Provincetown	58th MA Reg't	kia, Cold Harbor, VA, June 3, 1864
14. Benson, Henry F.	Sandwich	45th MA Reg't	dow, Kinston, NC, Dec. 28, 1862
15. Besse, Henry J.	Falmouth	3rd MA Cav'y	dod, New Orleans, Aug. 8, 1864
16. Blagden, James R.	Barnstable	58th MA Reg't	dow, Cold Harbor, June 11, 1864
17. Blake, David A.	Sandwich	1st ME Cav'y	dow, Maine, Feb. 13, 1862
18. Blauvelt, James Sr.	Chatham	39th MA Reg't	dod, Washington, DC, Dec. 9, 1863
19. Bolton, John	Chatham	58th MA Reg't	kia, Cold Harbor, June 3, 1864
20. Bourne, Isaac D.	Sandwich	5th RI Reg't	dod, Beaufort, NC, May 22, 1864
21. Bourne, Samuel	Falmouth	8th MI Reg't	dod, Brewster, Sept. 8, 1864
22. Brimmer, John	Wellfleet	41st MA Reg't	dod, Fort Hamilton, NY, Feb. 16, 1863
23. Bryant, William R.	Wellfleet	1st MA Cav'y	dow, U.S. Navy, Feb. 17, 1865
24. Burgess, Joshua T.	Harwich	58th MA Reg't	dod, Salisbury, NC, prison, Jan. 25, 1865
25. Burt, Jonathan	Barnstable	30th MA Reg't	dod, New Orleans, June 3, 1862
26. Cahoon, Obed A.	Barnstable	40th MA Reg't	dod, Beaufort, SC, Nov. 21, 1863
27. Cahoon, Simeon	Harwich	58th MA Reg't	dow, Wilderness, July 10, 1864

Cape Cod Civil War Deaths

Name	Town	Unit	Circumstances
28. Chase, Braddock R.	Falmouth	30th MA Reg't	dod, Ship Island, MS, May 20, 1862
29. Chase, Isaiah II	Harwich	58th MA Reg't	dod, Washington, DC, June 14, 1864
30. Chase, John S.	Dennis	58th MA Reg't	dow, Cold Harbor, Sept. 24, 1864
31. Chase, Kelly Jr.	Dennis	40th MA Reg't	dod, Portsmouth, VA, Oct. 1, 1864
32. Chase, Thomas B.	Harwich	58th MA Reg't	dod, Danville, VA, prison, Feb. 9, 1865
33. Childs, George W.	Barnstable	56th MA Reg't	dow, N. Anna, VA, June 11, 1864
34. Childs, Job F.	Barnstable	14th MA Batt'y	dod, City Point, VA, June 27, 1864
35. Childs, Simeon Jr.	Barnstable	14th MA Batt'y	dod, Beverly, NJ, Oct. 3, 1864
36. Chipman, Charles	Sandwich	29th MA Reg't	dow, Petersburg, VA, Aug. 7, 1864
37. Chipman, Wm. H.	Provincetown	1st Mar. Art'y	(no death information)
38. Cobb, Andrew P.	Barnstable	3rd MA Cav'y	dow, Sabine Pass, TX, Sept. 8, 1863
39. Coleman, Thomas Jr.	Barnstable	58th MA Reg't	prisoner, July 30, 1864 (no further info)
40. Cook, Barnabas Jr.	Truro	26th MA Reg't	dod, Salisbury, NC, prison, Dec. 9, 1864
41. Cook, Charles G.	Barnstable	58th MA Reg't	dod, Danville, VA, prison, Feb. 3, 1865
42. Cowan, John H.	Orleans	15th MA Reg't	dow, Wilderness, May 24, 1864
43. Crabbe, Alvah B.	Harwich	58th MA Reg't	dow, Cold Harbor, June 19, 1864
44. Crocker, Enoch	Barnstable	11th MA Reg't	dow, first Bull Run, July 21, 1861

Name	Town	Unit	Circumstances
45. Crocker, George E.	Provincetown	29th MA Reg't	dod, Provincetown, Feb. 14, 1863
46. Crocker, Horace L.	Barnstable	13th MA Reg't	dod, Bull Run, VA, March 30, 1862
47. Crocker, Zenas B.	Barnstable	90th NY Reg't	dod, Baton Rouge, LA, Aug. 14, 1863
48. Crosby, Edmund Jr.	Brewster	40th MA Reg't	dod, Andersonville, Aug. 25, 1864
49. Crowell, Isaac B.	Yarmouth	13th MA Reg't	kia, second Bull Run, Aug. 30, 1862
50. Dalton, James	Sandwich	24th MA Reg't	dod, Sandwich, Aug. 23, 1867
51. Davis, Benjamin	Sandwich	20th MA Reg't	kia, Balls Bluff, VA, Oct. 21, 1861
52. Dill, Zebina H.	Chatham	58th MA Reg't	dod, Andersonville, Aug. 28, 1864
53. Dillingham, Charles	Brewster	2nd MA Reg't	dow, Cedar Mountain, Sept. 10, 1862
54. Doane, Eliphalet	Barnstable	58th MA Reg't	kia, Petersburg, VA, June 20, 1864
55. Doane, Everett W.	Harwich	58th MA Reg't	kia, Petersburg, VA, April 2, 1865
56. Doane, Francis L.	Harwich	58th MA Reg't	dod, Andersonville, Sept. 1864
57. Doane, Moses	Harwich	58th MA Reg't	dow, Spotsylvania, Aug. 21, 1865
58. Doane, Solomon N.	Harwich	58th MA Reg't	dod, Andersonville, Aug. 24, 1864
59. Doty, Timothy F.	Falmouth	38th MA Reg't	dod, Baton Rouge, LA, Aug. 23, 1863
60. Drown, Alvan L.	Eastham	58th MA Reg't	dod, Harwich, Sept. 1, 1864
61. Drury, James	Provincetown	56th MA Reg't	died as POW, Millen, Georgia

Cape Cod Civil War Deaths

Name	Town	Unit	Circumstances
62. Dustin, Benjamin F.	Yarmouth	1st ME Batt'y	dod, New Orleans, Aug. 29, 1862
63. Eldredge, Alpheus	Harwich	58th MA Reg't	dow, Washington, DC, June 15, 1864
64. Eldredge, Lewis	Orleans	unknown	listed on Orleans Civil War monument
65. Eldridge, Augustus	Chatham	26th MA Reg't	dod, New Orleans, Sept. 3, 1863
66. Eldridge, Ebenezer	Barnstable	58th MA Reg't	kia, Spotsylvania, May 10, 1864
67. Eldridge, George S.	Brewster	58th MA Reg't	dod, Brewster, Feb. 13, 1865
68. Eldridge, John B.	Harwich	51st IL Reg't	kia, Kennesaw Mountain, GA, Jun 20, 1864
69. Eldridge, Nathan	Chatham	58th MA Reg't	kia, Spotsylvania, May 12, 1864
70. Ellis, Nathaniel S.	Sandwich	40th MA Reg't	dod, Philadelphia, July 19, 1864
71. Ellis, Thomas	Sandwich	40th MA Reg't	dod, Point of Rocks, VA, Aug. 13, 1864
72. Ellis, Warren H.	Yarmouth	5th MA Reg't	dod, Yarmouth, Sept. 22, 1863
73. Emerson, William L.	Sandwich	22nd MA Reg't	kia, Petersburg, VA, June 18, 1864
74. Ewer, Henry Jr.	Barnstable	24th MA Reg't	dod, Barnstable Village, Dec. 31, 1863
75. Finney, Alfred C.	Barnstable	5th MA Reg't	dod, New Bern, NC, March 31, 1863
76. Fish, Alvin N.	Falmouth	33rd MA Reg't	dow, Resaca, GA, May 30, 1864
77. Fish, Cyrus B.	Barnstable	40th MA Reg't	dod, Florence, SC, prison, Feb. 1865

Name	Town	Unit	Circumstances
78. Fish, George W.	Falmouth	38th MA Reg't	dod, Baton Rouge, LA, Aug. 7, 1863
79. Fish, Jehiel H.	Falmouth	38th MA Reg't	dod, New Orleans, June 28, 1863
80. Fish, John F.	Sandwich	24th MA Reg't	dod, South Sandwich, Oct. 5, 1862
81. Fish, Josiah C.	Barnstable	6th ME Reg't	kia, Rappahannock Station, VA, Nov. 7, 1863
82. Fish, Rufus H.	Falmouth	33rd MA Reg	kia, Wauhatchie, TN, Oct. 29, 1863
83. Foster, Augustus E.	Falmouth	38th MA Reg't	dow, Port Hudson, LA, June 21, 1863
84. Freeman, William N.	Sandwich	1st MA Reg't	dod, Philadelphia, Jan. 5, 1863
85. Fuller, Benjamin	Barnstable	29th MA Reg't	dod, W. Barnstable, Aug. 22, 1864
86. Gaffney, James	Sandwich	11th MA Reg't	dod, Andersonville, July 30, 1864
87. Gibbs, Thomas M.	Sandwich	61st MA Reg't	dod, Washington, DC, July 5, 1865
88. Gibbons, Thomas J.	Provincetown	3rd MA Cav'y	dow, Port Hudson LA, Nov. 10, 1863
89. Gifford, Jonathan	Harwich	40th MA Reg't	dod, Andersonville, Aug. 1, 1864
90. Godfrey, Charles N.	Sandwich	11th NH Reg't	dod, New York, NY, July 19, 1864
91. Gould, Joshua	Orleans	24th MA Reg't	dod, New York, NY, April 4, 1864
92. Graves, Ezekiel B.	Falmouth	13th MA Batt'y	dod, New Orleans, Oct. 31, 1864
93. Haines, James G.B.	Sandwich	29th MA Reg't	dod, Sandwich, July 26, 1862
94. Hall, Daniel M.	Wellfleet	2nd MA Cav'y	dod, Florence, SC, prison, Aug. 7, 1864

Cape Cod Civil War Deaths

Name	Town	Unit	Circumstances
95. Hall, Freeman Jr.	Harwich	58th MA Reg't	kia, Spotsylvania, VA, May 12, 1864
96. Hammond, Frank D.	Chatham	58th MA Reg't	kia, Petersburg, VA, June 23, 1864
97. Hammond, Luther	Sandwich	40th MA Reg't	dod, Beaufort, SC, Dec. 25, 1863
98. Handy, Moses A.	Harwich	58th MA Reg't	dod, Andersonville, Sept. 30, 1864
99. Harley, William H.	Chatham	58th MA Reg't	kia, Spotsylvania, VA, May 12, 1864
100. Hathaway, James A.	Barnstable	39th MA Reg't	dod, Salisbury, NC, prison, Jan. 10, 1865
101. Heald, James H.	Sandwich	29th MA Reg't	dod, Annapolis, MD, Oct. 9. 1862
102. Heffernan, Edward	Sandwich	3rd MA Cav'y	kia, Fishers Hill, VA, Sept. 22, 1864
103. Higgins, Solomon	Provincetown	56th MA Reg't	dod, Provincetown, March 9, 1864
104. Hill, George W.	Falmouth	38th MA Reg't	dod, Andersonville, July 22, 1864
105. Hoben, John W.	Provincetown	56th MA Reg't	kia, Peebles Farm, VA, Sept. 30, 1864
106. Holbrook, William A.	Wellfleet	4th MA Batt'y	dod, Franklin, LA, Jan. 29, 1864
107. Holway, Roland G.	Sandwich	58th MA Reg't	dod, Washington, DC, Aug. 14, 1864
108. Hopkins, Daniel P.	Eastham	43rd MA Reg't	dod, Eastham, July 16, 1863
109. Hopkins, John L.D.	Truro	58th MA Reg't	dod, Salisbury, NC, prison, Feb. 10, 1865
110. Howes, Seth T.	Chatham	58th MA Reg't	kia, Wilderness May 6, 1864
111. Howes, Stephen R.	Dennis	58th MA Reg't	dow, Wilderness, June 23, 1864

Name	Town	Unit	Circumstances
112. Jenkins, Nathan T.	Falmouth	19th MA Reg't	dod as pow, Richmond, VA, Dec. 4, 1863
113. Jones, Charles E.	Sandwich	29th MA Reg't	died of injuries in Virginia, Feb. 10, 1862
114. Jones, Ezra S.	Falmouth	38th MA Reg't	dod, Carrollton, LA, Jan. 12, 1863
115. Johnson, Lewis	Provincetown	11th MA Reg't	kia, Petersburg, VA, Sept. 10, 1864
116. Kelley, Adelbert	Barnstable	20th MA Reg't	dod, Centerville, MA, Aug. 26, 1865
117. Kelley, Silas N.	Dennis	58th MA Reg't	dod, David's Island, NY, June 28, 1864
118. Kelley, William B.	Harwich	39th MA Reg't	dow, Philadelphia, August 1864
119. King, Joseph	Provincetown	56th MA Reg't	dod, Salisbury, NC, prison, Nov. 16, 1864
120. Knippe, Henry H.	Sandwich	1st MA Cav'y	dod, Andersonville, Aug. 8, 1864
121. Landers, Joseph N.	Falmouth	41st MA Reg't	dod, Baton Rouge, March 20, 1863
122. Lawrence, Edward J.	Sandwich	40th MA Reg't	dod, Folly Island, SC, Nov. 26, 1863
123. Lewis, Horace E.	Falmouth	38th MA Reg't	dod, Brashear City, LA, June 1, 1863
124. Linnell, Shubael	Barnstable	3rd MA Cav'y	dod, Salisbury, NC, prison, Nov. 28, 1864
125. Lockwood, George	Provincetown	2nd MA Art'y	dod, New Bern, NC, Nov. 28, 1864
126. Lombard, Benjamin K.	Truro	58th MA Reg't	dod, Andersonville, July 11, 1864
127. Long, Patrick	Sandwich	29th MA Reg't	dod, Newport News, VA, Aug. 9, 1862

Name	Town	Unit	Circumstances
128. Lumbert, William L.	Barnstable	40th MA Reg't	dod, Beaufort, SC, Jan. 1, 1864
129. Lurton, John C.	Provincetown	56th MA Reg't	kia, Petersburg, VA, July 30, 1864
130. Lyman, Charles	Chatham	18th MA Reg't	dod, Chatham, May 21, 1863
131. Maker, Samuel	Brewster	58th MA Reg't	dow, Wilderness, May 6, 1864
132. Marchant, Allen	Barnstable	58th MA Reg't	dod, Hyannis, April 1866
133. Marvel, Samuel M.	Sandwich	58th MA Reg't	dod, Salisbury, NC prison, Dec. 29, 1864
134. Matthews, Ferdinand	Yarmouth	23rd MA Reg't	dod, Newbern, NC, June 9, 1862
135. Matthews, William H.	Yarmouth	35th MA Reg't	dod, Aquia Creek, VA, Feb. 7, 1863
136. McKenna, Peter	Sandwich	20th MA Reg't	kia, Balls Bluff, VA, Oct. 21, 1861
137. McKowen, James	Sandwich	3rd MA Cav'y	died, 1865 (circumstances unknown)
138. Morgan, William H.	Sandwich	2nd MA Cav'y	dow, Woodstock, VA, Sept. 22, 1864
139. Morrill, Charles W.	Wellfleet	30th MA Reg't	dod, Baton Rouge, Aug. 6, 1862
140. Morrison, Henry T.	Eastham	33rd MA Reg't	dow, Resaca, GA, May 16, 1864
141. Murphy, John	Sandwich	56th MA Reg't	dod, Readville, MA, March 1864
142. Nelson, Charles	Barnstable	6th ME Reg't	kia, Rappahannock Station, VA, Nov. 7, 1863
143. Nicholson, John A.	Barnstable	56th MA Reg't	dow, Wilderness, May 31, 1864

Name	Town	Unit	Circumstances
144. Nickerson, Edwin	Chatham	58th MA Reg't	dod, Danville, VA, prison, Jan. 27, 1865
145. Nickerson, Samuel	Eastham	58th MA Reg't	kia, Petersburg, VA, Jan. 7, 1865
146. Nye, Ephraim B.	Sandwich	14th MA Bat'y	kia, Fort Stedman, VA, March 25, 1865
147. Nye, Walter S.	Falmouth	38th MA Reg't	dod, Baton Rouge, April 19, 1863
148. O'Neil, James	Sandwich	9th MA Reg't	kia, Spotsylvania, May 8, 1864
149. Otis, Samuel B.	Barnstable	40th MA Reg't	dod, Beaufort, SC, Nov. 16, 1863
150. Otis, Solomon	Barnstable	40th MA Reg't	kia, Drurys Bluff, VA, May 16, 1864
151. Packard, Charles M.	Sandwich	11th RI Reg't	dod, Monument, MA, Oct. 30, 1866
152. Paine, Jeremiah T.	Truro	39th MA Reg't	dod, Washington, DC, Oct. 12, 1863
153. Pendergrass, James	Barnstable	58th MA Reg't	dod, Salisbury, NC prison, Dec. 20, 1864
154. Penniman, Francis	Eastham	33rd MA Reg't	dow, Kennesaw Mountain, GA, July 8, 1864
155. Perry, George R.	Sandwich	95th PA Reg't	kia, Chancellorsville, VA, May 1863
156. Phillips, Franklin	Harwich	122nd NY Reg't	dow, Cold Harbor, June 3, 1864
157. Phinney, Albro W.	Barnstable	125th PA Reg't	dod, Loudoun Valley, VA, Nov. 10, 1862
158. Phinney, William W.	Sandwich	1st MA Cav'y	dod, near Fortress Monroe, April 1, 1865
159. Pitcher, Nathan A.	Barnstable	40th MA Reg't	dod, Folly Island, SC, Nov. 14, 1863

Name	Town	Unit	Circumstances
160. Robbins, Timothy	Barnstable	58th MA Reg't	dod, Salisbury, NC, prison, Dec. 29, 1864
161. Rogers, Charles A.	Orleans	25th MA Reg't	kia, New Bern, NC, March 14, 1862
162. Rogers, David N.	Brewster	4th MA Bat'y	dod, Nantucket, March 14, 1864
163. Ryder, Amos C.	Dennis	58th MA Reg't	dow, Cold Harbor, June 24, 1864
164. Ryder, John C.	Truro	58th MA Reg't	missing, May 5, 1864. (more information not available)
165. Shiverick, Andrew T.	Falmouth	28th WI Reg't	dod, Memphis, TN, April 22, 1863
166. Scudder, Joseph C.	Barnstable	40th MA Reg't	dod, Osterville, May 3, 1864
167. Shaw, Colin	Sandwich	11th MA Reg't	dow, Gettysburg, Aug. 6, 1863
168. Small, Taylor Jr.	Provincetown	56th MA Reg't	dod, Danville, VA prison, Feb. 5, 1865
169. Smalley, Ebenezer	Harwich	58th MA Reg't	dow, Petersburg, July 11, 1864
170. Smalley, Elisha F.	Dennis	5th CT Reg't	dod, Baltimore, Oct. 2, 1861
171. Smith, Elkanah K.	Eastham	56th MA Reg't	dod, Annapolis, MD, Oct. 26, 1864
172. Smith, Henry A.F.	Provincetown	12th MA Reg't	dow, Petersburg, VA, July 19, 1864
173. Smith, Isaac Y.	Orleans	43rd MA Reg't	kia, White Hall, NC, Dec. 16, 1864
174. Smith, James W.	Eastham	24th MA Reg't	dod, New Bern, NC, April 3, 1862
175. Smith, John R.	Provincetown	56th MA Reg't	dod, Philadelphia, June 25, 1864

Name	Town	Unit	Circumstances
176. Smith, Nathaniel B.	Chatham	58th MA Reg't	kia, Cold Harbor, VA, June 3, 1864
177. Smith, Stephen	Harwich	58th MA Reg't	kia, Wilderness, VA, May 6, 1864
178. Snow, Franklin	Yarmouth	94th IL Reg't	dod, New Orleans, Aug. 23, 1863
179. Sparrow, William E.	Orleans	43rd MA Reg't	kia, Goldsboro, NC, Dec. 17, 1862
180. Spencer, George Jr.	Chatham	58th MA Reg't	dod, Salisbury, NC, prison, Jan. 26, 1865
181. Studley, Ansel L.	Dennis	58th MA Reg't	dod, Dennis, Oct. 25, 1864
182. Studley, James F.	Orleans	33rd MA Reg't	dod, Alexandria, VA, March 19, 1864
183. Swift, Dean W.	Sandwich	40th MA Reg't	dow, Drurys Bluff, Jun 23, 1864
184. Swift, Joseph H.	Falmouth	24th MA Reg't	dod, Sandwich, Feb. 17, 1865
185. Thorndike, Jeremiah	Provincetown	12th MA Reg't	dod, Alexandria, VA, Nov. 15, 1863
186. Tinkham, Martin S.	Barnstable	29th MA Reg't	dod, Fortress Monroe, VA, Sept. 27, 1861
187. Tupper, William E.	Provincetown	1st Mar. Art'y	dod, New Bern, NC, July 18, 1862
188. Upham, Charles M.	Chatham	58th MA Reg't	kia, Cold Harbor, VA, June 3, 1864
189. Walker, John W.	Orleans	4th MA Cav'y	dod, Hilton Head, SC, July 16, 1864
190. Ward, James	Sandwich	36th MA Reg't	kia, Spotsylvania, May 12, 1864
191. Weeks, John	Sandwich	29th MA Reg't	dod, Hampton, VA, Oct. 20, 1861
192. Weeks, Willard	Sandwich	40th MA Reg't	dod, Fortress Monroe, VA, Jan. 23, 1865

Cape Cod Civil War Deaths

Name	Town	Unit	Circumstances
193. Wetherbee, Gardner	Brewster	47th MA Reg't	dod, New Orleans, April 23, 1863
194. Wheeler, Thomas Jr.	Sandwich	28th MA Reg't	kia, second Bull Run, VA, Aug. 30, 1862
195. Wilson, James B.	Barnstable	20th MA Reg't	dow, Wilderness, June 1, 1864
196. Wing, Gideon	Sandwich	7th IN Cav'y	kia, Guntown, MS, June 12, 1864
197. Winslow, Edward	Truro	20th MA Reg't	dod, Washington, DC, May 23, 1862
198. Winslow, Nathan	Barnstable	35th MA Reg't	dow, Antietam, Nov. 25, 1862
199. Wixon, Amos F.	Dennis	58th MA Reg't	kia, Cold Harbor, VA, June 3, 1864
200. Wixon, Benjamin F.	Brewster	58th MA Reg't	dow, Spotsylvania, May 13, 1864
201. Wood, Samuel J.	Sandwich	40th MA Reg't	dod, Petersburg, VA, Aug. 21, 1864
202. Wood, William H.	Sandwich	29th MA Reg't	dod, Newport News, VA, Jan. 16, 1862
203. Woodward, Ezekiel	Sandwich	20th MA Reg't	dow, Fredricksburg, Dec. 13, 1862
204. Young, Aaron H.	Barnstable	45th MA Reg't	dow, Goldsboro, NC, Jan. 20, 1863
205. Young, David G.	Chatham	58th MA Reg't	dow, Wilderness, May 11, 1864

NOTES

1. ABOLITION AND POLITICS

1. Stacey M. Robertson, "'A Hard, Cold, Stern Life': Parker Pillsbury and Grassroots Abolitionism 1840–1865." *New England Quarterly* 70, no. 2 (June 1997): 180.
2. *Liberator*, February 9, 1838; Beth A. Salerno, *Sister Societies: Women's Antislavery Organizations in Antebellum America* (DeKalb: Northern Illinois University Press, 2005), 28 and 168.
3. *Barnstable Patriot*, November 19, 1845.
4. *Liberator*, "Anti-Slavery Tour on the Cape," February 21, 1845; *Liberator*, February 28, 1845.
5. *Liberator*, November 6, 1846; *Liberator*, November 13, 1846; *Liberator*, February 26, 1847; *Liberator*, "Anti-Slavery Conventions," March 19, 1847.
6. *Barnstable Patriot*, "The Fourth of July," July 7, 1847; *Liberator*, September 3, 1847; *Liberator*, October 1, 1847.
7. *Liberator*, February 11, 1848; *Liberator*, February 18, 1848; *Liberator*, March 17, 1848; *Liberator*, "Anti-Slavery FAIR!" December 8, 1848.
8. Parker Pillsbury to Helen Pillsbury, February 22, 1848.
9. *Liberator*, August 20, 1847; *Liberator*, September 1, 1848; *Barnstable Patriot*, August 23, 1848; Robertson, "'A Hard, Cold, Stern Life,'" 194.
10. *Liberator*, September 8, 1848; *Liberator*, September 15, 1848; *Liberator*, September 22, 1848.
11. *Barnstable Patriot*, "Shoot-Flying Hill," September 6, 1848.
12. *Barnstable Patriot*, October 11, 1848.
13. *Barnstable Patriot*, November 15, 1848.
14. *Liberator*, "Visit to Cape Cod," September 21, 1849; *Liberator*, "To the Abolitionists of Cape Cod," November 23, 1849; *Liberator*, "Anti-Slavery in Barnstable County," December 14, 1849.
15. *Liberator*, "Barnstable County A.S. Society," January 25, 1850.
16. *Barnstable Patriot*, January 15, 1850; *Barnstable Patriot*, Kies Doane Obituary, February 26, 1895. Catherine H. Doane died in 1857.
17. *Liberator*, "Falmouth," September 8, 1851; *Liberator*, "Anti-Slavery Labor in Harwich and Brewster," August 27, 1852; *Liberator*, "Anti-Slavery Expression on the Cape," September 3, 1852.
18. Stanley W. Campbell, *The Slave Catchers: Enforcement of the Fugitive Slave Law 1850–1860* (New York: W.W. Norton Co., 1972); *Liberator*, April 11, 1851; Austin Bearse, *Reminiscences of Fugitive-Slave Days in Boston* (Boston: privately printed, 1880), 23; *Barnstable Patriot*, "The Fugitive Slave Case," April 8, 1851.

19. *Boston Daily Advertiser*, April 13, 1851; *Liberator*, March 21, 1851; *Liberator*, April 11, 1851; *Liberator*, April 18, 1851; Simeon Deyo, *History of Barnstable County* (New York: H.W. Blake. 1890), 445; *Barnstable Patriot*, "Surrender of Sims to His Claimant," April 15, 1851; *Barnstable Patriot*, December 7, 1880. According to *Barnstable Patriot*, March 5, 1913, Marston's first Boston restaurant was established in 1847 on Commercial Street.
20. *Liberator*, September 15, 1848; *Liberator*, April 11, 1851.
21. *Liberator*, "Benj. F. Hallett's Welcome Home," August 11, 1854.
22. *Liberator*, "Anti-Slavery Labor in Harwich and Brewster," August 27, 1852.
23. *Barnstable Patriot*, July 15, 1856.
24. *Barnstable Patriot*, July 29, 1856; *Barnstable Patriot*, September 9, 1856; *Barnstable Patriot*, September 23, 1856; *Liberator*, April 29, 1859.
25. *Barnstable Patriot*, November 18, 1856; *Barnstable Patriot*, November 25, 1856.
26. *Barnstable Patriot*, November 18, 1856.
27. *Barnstable Patriot*, September 2, 1856; *Barnstable Patriot*, April 7, 1857.
28. *New York Times*, "The Hyannis Kidnapping Case," June 1, 1859; *Barnstable Patriot*, November 21, 1859; *Boston Daily Advertiser*, November 21, 1859.
29. *Liberator*, June 17, 1859; *Liberator*, "Anti-Slavery Labors on the Cape," October 12, 1860.
30. Sears Diary; *Liberator*, December 16, 1859.
31. *Barnstable Patriot*, January 3, 1860.
32. *Liberator*, March 25, 1859; *Liberator*, March 30, 1860; *New York Times*, January 24, 1861.
33. *Barnstable Patriot*, March 30, 1842; *Barnstable Patriot*, (Mary Dunn) April 20, 1842; *Barnstable Patriot*, November 12, 1850; *Barnstable Patriot*, April 21, 1913; Marriage records of Alvan Howes, Massachusetts State Archives, Boston.
34. *Barnstable Patriot*, "Chicago Convention," May 22, 1860; *Barnstable Patriot*, "A Defeated Candidate," May 29, 1860; *Yarmouth Register*, "The Organ on Intellectual Matters," June 8, 1860.
35. *Barnstable Patriot*, September 18, 1860; *Yarmouth Register*, October 5, 1860; *Boston Daily Advertiser*, October 4, 1860.
36. *Barnstable Patriot*, November 13, 1860; *Barnstable Patriot*, November 20, 1860.
37. Internal improvements (extension of C. Cod Railroad) were also a factor in the strong Lincoln vote.

2. First Blood

1. *Barnstable Patriot*, "Clearances from the Port of Charleston," January 22, 1861.
2. The War of the Rebellion: A Compilation of the Official Records of the Union and Confederate Armies, series 1, vol. 1, 345–347; *Joseph Whitney* Vessel Files, National Archives Records Group 92, entry 1403, box 115, National Archives, Washington, D.C.
3. War of the Rebellion, 522–598; *Star of the West* Vessel Files, box 101, National Archives, Washington, D.C.; Mrs. Samuel Posey, "Capture of the Star of the West," *Confederate Veteran* 32 (May 1924): 74; *Barnstable Patriot*, April 23, 1861. This was the same *Star of the West* sent to Fort Sumter in January in a resupply mission. Howes was not the captain for that voyage. The result of Howes's protest is unknown.
4. *Barnstable Patriot*, "Arrivals, Clearances, Etc.," February 12, 1861; *Barnstable Patriot*, "Arrivals, Clearances, Etc.," March 12, 1861; *Barnstable Patriot*, "From the South," June 11, 1861.
5. *Barnstable Patriot*, "Cape Cod Lodge," February 19, 1861; *Barnstable Patriot*, April 16, 1861; *Boston Daily Courier*, "Charleston Steamers," February 27, 1861; Alfred S. Roe, *The Fifth Regiment Massachusetts Volunteer Infantry* (Boston: Fifth Regiment Veterans Association, 1911), 8.

6. Robert F. Magraw, "Minutement of '61: The Pre-Civil War Massachusetts Militia," *Civil War History* 15, no. 1 (June 1969): 101–115; William Schouler, *A History of Massachusetts in the Civil War* (Boston: E.P. Dutton and Co., 1868), 48–49.

7. *Barnstable Patriot*, "Captain Eldridge and the Secessionists," April 30, 1861; *Barnstable Patriot*, May 7, 1861: *Lowell Daily Citizen and News*, April 18, 1861; *Philadelphia Inquirer*, April 25, 1861.

8. George W. Nason, *Minutemen of '61* (Boston: Smith and McCance, 1910), 2; *Barnstable Patriot*, April 30, 1861; Roe, *Fifth Regiment*, 30, 361–365.

9. *Barnstable Patriot*, April 23, 1861; *Barnstable Patriot*, April 30, 1861; *Yarmouth Register*, May 3, 1861.

10. *New Bedford Republican Standard*, May 9, 1861; Maria Withington Jones Diary, New Bedford Whaling Museum, New Bedford, Massachusetts; *Middleboro Gazette*, May 25, 1861; *Barnstable Patriot*, May 28, 1861; *Barnstable Patriot*, June 18, 1861; Shebnah Rich. *Truro Cape Cod or Landmarks and Seamarks* (Boston: D. Lothrop and Co., 1884), 473.

11. *Barnstable Patriot*, June 26, 1860; *Barnstable Patriot*, July 17, 1860.

12. *Barnstable Patriot*, May 14, 1861; *Barnstable Patriot*, May 21, 1861.

13. *Barnstable Patriot*, "Celebration of the Fourth at Wellfleet," July 9, 1861; *Barnstable Patriot*, "The Fourth," July 16, 1861; Jones Diary. Just who or what the Horribles were is unclear. Perhaps they were marchers in grotesque masks and outfits.

14. Miscellaneous Letters Received by the Secretary of the Navy, microfilm 124, roll 372, National Archives, Washington, D.C.; *Barnstable Patriot*, May 14, 1861; *Barnstable Patriot*, May 21, 1861.

15. *Barnstable Patriot*, "Escape of an Osterville Vessel," April 30, 1861; *Barnstable Patriot*, "How a Northern Shipmaster was Treated at Norfolk," May 14, 1861.

16. *Yarmouth Register*, May 17, 1861; *Yarmouth Register*, May 31, 1861; *New York Times*, May 30, 1861; *Falmouth Enterprise*, July 7, 1961; *Falmouth Enterprise*, August 11, 1961; *Falmouth Enterprise*, September 11, 1961; Samuel F. Du Pont Correspondence, September 1861, Hagley Museum and Library, Wilmington, Delaware. Mosquito Inlet is present-day Daytona Beach.

17. Official Records of the Union and Confederate Navies in the War of the Rebellion (ORN), series 1, vol. 4, 345; *Barnstable Patriot*, "Seizure of the Ship Abaelino," June 4, 1861; William Robinson Jr., *The Confederate Privateers* (New Haven: Yale University Press, 1928), 43; *New Orleans Times Picayune*, February 19, 1863.

18. *Barnstable Patriot*, June 11, 1861; *Yarmouth Register*, June 14, 1861.

19. Edward T. Cotham, *Battle on the Bay: The Civil War Struggle of Galveston* (Austin: University of Texas Press, 1998), 27; *Barnstable Patriot*, "Marine List," April 18, 1861; *Barnstable Patriot*, "Another Seizure by the Rebels," June 18, 1861; *Barnstable Patriot*, "Deaths," July 23, 1861.

20. *New York Times*, "The Pirates," August 26, 1861; *Barnstable Patriot*, "Seizure of a Sandwich Schooner," August 27, 1861; ORN, series 1, vol. 1, 65.

21. ORN, series 1, vol. 1, 67; *Barnstable Patriot*, July 23, 1861; *Barnstable Patriot*, July 30, 1861; *Barnstable Patriot*, August 13, 1861.

22. *Yarmouth Register*, June 20, 1862; *Barnstable Patriot*, June 24, 1862; *Barnstable Patriot*, April 15, 1912; *Barnstable Patriot*, March 3, 1938; Herbert Manton Vessel Files, box 60, National Archives, Washington, D.C.; ORN, series 1, vol. 2, 289.

23. *New York Herald*, July 21, 1861; *New York Tribune*, September 25, 1861; ORN, series 1, vol. 1, 51; *Barnstable Patriot*, July 22, 1862.

24. ORN, series 1, vol. 16, 575; ORN, series 1, vol. 6, 17 and 71; ORN, series 1, vol. 1, 60; *New York Times*, "Privateering—The Case of the George G. Baker," August 15, 1861; Robinson, *Confederate Privateers*, 105. Baxter's awkward position with the *South Carolina* may explain his brief stay in the navy.

25. *Yarmouth Register*, July 26, 1861; *Yarmouth Register*, August 2, 1861; *Barnstable Patriot*, July 23, 1861; *Boston Daily Courier*, July 24, 1861; *New York Times*, August 11, 1861.

3. CAPE COD AND THE NAVY

1. Robert B. Forbes Diary, box 4, and letters, box 3, folder 2, Massachusetts History Society. Boston, Massachusetts.

2. Robert B. Forbes, *Personal Reminiscences* (Boston: Little Brown, 1878), 258–284; *Barnstable Patriot*, July 9 and 16, 1861. In 1863, Evander White of Hyannis's White House Hotel asked for and received an eighty-dollar reimbursement for "hospitality" extended during the coast guard visit.

3. Miscellaneous Letters, National Archives Record Group 45, microfilm 209, roll 23; Forbes, *Personal Reminiscences*, 258–284.

4. ORN, series 1, vol. 1, 44–45; Robinson, *Confederate Privateers*, 311–315. By international law, a blockade has to be an effective one. Otherwise, it and the blockaded entity are subject to foreign intervention.

5. *Washington Daily Globe*, July 18, 1861.

6. Paul H. Silverstone, *Civil War Navies 1855–1883* (Annapolis: Naval Institute Press, 2001), 105–106; *New York Times*, November 4, 1860; *Barnstable Patriot*, September 22, 1857; *Barnstable Patriot*, July 16, 1861.

7. *Barnstable Patriot*, January 14, 1862.

8. *Barnstable Patriot*, January 21, 1861; *Barnstable Patriot*, July 22, 1862.

9. Miscellaneous Letters, microfilm 124, roll 400.

10. *Barnstable Patriot*, March 4, 1862; *Yarmouth Register*, February 21, 1862.

11. *Boston Evening Journal*, January 28, 1862; Letters Received by the Secretary of the Navy from Officers Below the Rank of Commander, microfilm 148, roll 297, National Archives, Washington, D.C.

12. *Barnstable Patriot*, September 20, 1864. A subject much in need of research is Cape Civil War Navy enlisted men.

13. Letters Received by Secretary of the Navy from Commanding Officers of Squadrons, microfilm 89, roll 138, National Archives, Washington, D.C.; Records Concerning Pilots, National Archives Record Group 45, entry 130, National Archives, Washington, D.C.; *Massachusetts Soldiers, Sailors and Marines of the Civil War*, vol. 7 (Norwood, MA: Norwood Press, 1933); *Barnstable Patriot*, October 22, 1861; *Barnstable Patriot*, December 10, 1861; *Barnstable Patriot*, January 14, 1862; *Barnstable Patriot*, February 25, 1862; *Barnstable Patriot*, April 21, 1863; *Yarmouth Register*, February 7, 1862; George W. Bacon, National Archives Pension Records.

14. ORN, series 1, vol. 8, 725, 759–760; ORN, series 1, vol. 9, 32; Records Concerning Pilots; Neva O'Neil, *Master Mariners of Dennis* (Dennis, MA: Dennis Historical Society, 1965), 13; *Barnstable Patriot*, Centerville News, June 3, 1895; *Barnstable Patriot*, Bourne News, June 6, 1893.

15. *Barnstable Patriot*, April 1, 1862; *Barnstable Patriot*, August 11, 1874. Precisely when Nickerson was pilot is unknown.

16. *Barnstable Patriot*, March 18, 1862.

17. "Brig *Sabao*," *The Reports of the Committees of the Senate of the United States*, 39th Cong., 1st sess., 1865–66; *Richmond Dispatch*, April 23, 1862; ORN, series 1, vol. 7, 223.

18. Frederick Phisterer, comp., *New York in the War of the Rebellion 1861–1865* (Albany, NY: Lyon Company. 1912), 1,541–42; *Hyannis Patriot*, February 3, 1938; *New York Herald*, February 15, 1862; *Barnstable Patriot*, February 25, 1862. Hawes Atwood stands unique among Cape Civil War servicemen, having served in the army, navy and marines.

19. *Barnstable Patriot*, February 25, 1862; *Barnstable Patriot*, July 22, 1862.

20. Dennis Ringle, *Life in Mr. Lincoln's Navy* (Annapolis: Naval Institute Press, 1998), 24.

4. THE TRANSPORTS

1. *Barnstable Patriot,* July 8, 1862.

2. *Charmer* Vessel Files, box 19, National Archives, Washington, D.C.; *Reindeer* Vessel Files, box 85, National Archives, Washington, D.C.

3. *Baltimore Sun*, April 29, 1861; *New York Herald*, May 7, 1861; *New York Herald*, July 14, 1861; ORN, series 1, vol. 6, 88.

4. Samuel F. Du Pont Correspondence, September 18, 1861 to January 19, 1862, Hagley Museum and Library, Wilmington, Delaware; *Boston Daily Courier*, December 16, 1861.

5. *New York Times*, January 29, 1862; *New York Herald*, January 30, 1862.

6. Daniel Larned Papers, Library of Congress, Washington, D.C.; *Barnstable Patriot*, February 25, 1862; *Boston Daily Courier*, February 22, 1862.

7. Senate Report 84, *Employment of Transport Vessels*, 37th Cong., 3rd sess., 1861-1863.

8. Georgeanna Woolsey Bacon, *Letters of a Family During the War, 1861–1865*, vol. 2 (privately printed, 1899), 367.

9. *Conquest* Vessel Files, box 23, National Archives, Washington, D.C.

10. *Boston Daily Evening Traveler*, January 20, 1862; *New York Times*, February 23, 1862; *Wild Gazelle* Vessel Files, box 37, National Archives, Washington, D.C.; *Young Turk* Vessel Files, box 108, National Archives, Washington, D.C.; *Daniel Webster* Vessel Files, box 113, National Archives, Washington, D.C. Part of the navy side of the expedition was Commodore David Porter's mortar schooner fleet, the one Cape seamen were so reluctant to join.

11. *Barnstable Patriot*, March 25, 1862; *Thomas W. House* Vessel Files, box 44, National Archives, Washington, D.C.

12. Du Pont Correspondence, March 30 to May 17, 1862; ORN, series 1, vol. 12, 374–378. The *Wilmington* (NC) *Morning Star* of March 10, 1992, reported the hull of the former *Commodore Hull* as still visible in North Carolina's Cape Fear River.

13. *Philadelphia Inquirer*, November 20, 1862; ORN, series 1, vol. 19, 241; *B. Delano* Vessel Files, box 27, National Archives, Washington, D.C.; *Julia Ford* Vessel Files, box 35, National Archives, Washington, D.C.; *New South*, December 6, 1862.

14. *Barnstable Patriot*, April 21, 1863; *Barnstable Patriot*, May 26, 1863; *New York Herald*, April 17, 1863.

15. *New York Times*, February 10, 1863; J. Henry Sears, *Brewster Ship Masters* (Yarmouthport, MA: C.W. Swift Publisher, 1906), 70; Alfred A. Doane, comp., The Doane Family and Their Descendants (Boston: Alfred A. Doane, 1902), 344.

16. John Chipman Gray and John Codman Ropes, *War Letters 1862–1865* (Boston: Houghton Mifflin, 1927), 172; George H. Gordon, *A War Diary of Events of the War of the Great Rebellion 1863–1865* (Boston: Osgood and Company, 1882), 456.

17. *E.M. Dyer* Vessel Files, box 31, National Archives, Washington, D.C.; *John Warner* Vessel Files, box 83, National Archives, Washington, D.C.; War of the Rebellion, series 1, vol. 36, part 2, 58; War of the Rebellion, series 1, vol. 35, part 1, 22.

18. *New York Times*, January 12, 1863.

19. *John Rice* Vessel Files, box 88, National Archives, Washington, D.C.; *Julia Smith* Vessel Files, box 98, National Archives, Washington, D.C.

20. *New York Herald*, May 8, 1864.

21. *New York Times*, July 26, 1864; War of the Rebellion, series 1, vol. 40, part 3, 221; War of the Rebellion, series 1, vol. 37, part 1, 273; *Ranger* Vessel Files, box 87, National Archives, Washington, D.C.

22. Edward H. Hall, "Reminiscences of the War: The Wilmington Expedition II," *United Service Magazine* 5, no. 1 (January 1866); *Barnstable Patriot*, March 28, 1865.

23. *Abby Bursley* Vessel Files, box 16, National Archives, Washington, D.C.; *S.A. Hammond* Vessel Files, box 41, National Archives, Washington, D.C.; *E. Nickerson* Vessel Files, box 76, National Archives, Washington, D.C.

24. *New York Tribune*, December 29, 1862; *Amazonian* Vessel Files, box 3, National Archives, Washington, D.C.; *Windermere* Vessel Files, box 115, National Archives, Washington, D.C.

25. *Exact* Vessel Files, box 33, National Archives, Washington, D.C.; War of the Rebellion, series 1, vol. 26, part 1, 296.

26. Gary D. Joiner, *Through the Howling Wilderness: The 1864 Red River Campaign and Union Failure in the West* (Knoxville: University of Tennessee Press, 2006), 150; *Barnstable Patriot*, May 24, 1864; *John Warner* Vessel Files, box 111, National Archives, Washington, D.C.

27. War of the Rebellion, series 1, vol. 48, part 2, 1,041; War of the Rebellion, series 1, vol. 49, part 2, 985; *Mystic* Vessel Files, box 73, National Archives, Washington, D.C.

5. Home Front and Front Line, 1861–62

1. *Barnstable Patriot*, October 22, 1861; *Barnstable Patriot*, November 12, 1861; Jones Diary, December 11–12, 1861.

2. *Yarmouth Register*, November 29, 1861; *Barnstable Patriot*, December 31, 1861.

3. Richard F. Miller, *Harvard's Civil War: A History of the Twentieth Massachusetts Volunteer Infantry* (Hanover, NH: University Press of New England, 2005), 33; Descriptive Books of the Twentieth Massachusetts Regiment, vol. 5, National Archives Record Group 94, National Archives, Washington, D.C.; Raymond E. Barlow and Joan E. Kaiser, *The Glass Industry in Sandwich*, vol. 3 (Windham, NH: Barlow-Kaiser Barlow Publishing Co., Inc., 1983), 23 and 98.

4. Francis W. Palfrey, *Memoir of William Francis Bartlett* (Cambridge: Riverside Press, 1878), 31–32; Peter McKenna and Thomas Hollis, National Archives Pension Records; "Extract of Letter from Thomas Hollis, submitted by his son, Thomas W. Hollis," 1896, MOLLUS Collection Harvard University, Cambridge, Massachusetts.

5. Terrence Murphy, Thomas Hollis and Thomas Davis, National Archives Pension Records; Miller, *Harvard's Civil War*, 178.

6. Phillip Riley, John F. Fish, Jesse H. Allen and William S. Washburn, National Archives Pension Records; Barnstable County Probate Records for Henry Ewer, 1861.

7. *Cape Cod Republican*, July 17, 1862. James B. McPherson became a famous Civil War general.

8. Martin S. Tinkham, National Archives Pension Records; *Barnstable Patriot*, October 8, 1861.

9. Willard Weeks and David A. Blake, National Archives Pension Records; Charles Chipman Letters, January 16, 1862, U.S. Army Heritage and Education Center, Carlisle, Pennsylvania; *Barnstable Patriot*, February 11, 1862.

10. Horace L. Crocker, Braddock Chase and Edward Winslow, National Archives Pension Records; *Barnstable Patriot*, November 26, 1861; *Barnstable Patriot*, Asa Crocker News, November 20, 1883; *Falmouth Enterprise*, August 1, 1961.

11. *Barnstable Patriot*, March 4, 1862; *Barnstable Patriot*, March 11, 1862.

12. *Cape Cod Republican*, February 20, 1862; *Barnstable Patriot*, February 25, 1862; *Barnstable Patriot*, May 27, 1862.

13. *Barnstable Patriot*, October 29, 1862; *Barnstable Patriot*, May 20, 1862; *Barnstable Patriot*, July 1, 1862; *New Bedford Daily Mercury*, November 19, 1861.

14. *Barnstable Patriot*, June 24, July 15 and 22, 1862 and June 9, 1883; Executive Letters, Massachusetts State Archives, Boston, Massachusetts.

15. Richard F. Miller, "For His Wife, His Widow, and His Orphan: Massachusetts and Family Aid During the Civil War." *Massachusetts Historical Review* 6 (2004), 71–106; *Barnstable Patriot*, July 29, 1862.

16. *Falmouth Enterprise*, July 21, 1961; *Postscripts* (newsletter of Bourne Historical Society), Fall 1991.

17. *Barnstable Patriot*, August 5, 1862; *Cape Cod Republican*, September 4, 1862; George N. Munsell, National Archives Pension Records.

18. *Falmouth Enterprise*, July 7, 1861; *Barnstable Patriot*, August 19, 1862; Executive Letters.

19. *Barnstable Patriot*, July 29, 1862; *Cape Cod Republican*, August 7, 1862; Joseph A. Nickerson Jr. and Louise D. Nickerson, *Chatham Sea Captains in the Age of Sail* (Charleston: The History Press, 2008), 56; Barnstable County Probate Records for James Blauvelt, 1864; Alfred S. Roe, *The Thirty-Ninth Regiment Massachusetts Volunteers 1862–1865* (Worchester, MA: privately printed, 1914), 338.

20. *Cape Cod Republican*, August 7, 1862; Roe, *Thirty-Ninth Regiment*, 25.

21. *Barnstable Patriot*, December 6, 1897; Cyrus B. Fish, National Archives Pension Records.

22. Andrea Leonard, Crocker Genealogy, vol. 2, B-8, Sturgis Library, Barnstable, Massachusetts.

23. *Yarmouth Register*, July 25, 1862; *Barnstable Patriot*, August 26, 1862. Lewis was in Company A.

24. *Barnstable Patriot*, July 29, 1862; James G.B. Haines, National Archives Pension Records.

25. *Barnstable Patriot*, August 26, 1862; *Barnstable Patriot*, September 2, 1862; *Barnstable Patriot*, September 9, 1862.

26. George L. Haines Letters, August 17, 1862, Sandwich Town Archives, Sandwich, Massachusetts.

27. *Barnstable Patriot*, August 26, 1862; *Barnstable Patriot*, September 9, 1862; Roe, *Fifth Regiment*, 398.

28. *Barnstable Patriot*, August 26, 1862; *Barnstable Patriot*, September 9, 1862; *Barnstable Patriot*, March 31, 1863; *Barnstable Patriot*, February 15, 1917; Roe, *Fifth Regiment*, 130.

29. *Barnstable Patriot*, August 26, 1862; *Barnstable Patriot*, September 2, 1862; *Barnstable Patriot*, September 16, 1862; *Cape Cod Republican*, September 18, 1862.

30. *Barnstable Patriot*, September 30, 1862.

31. *Barnstable Patriot*, September 2, 1862. The Readville camp was near Dedham.

32. *Barnstable Patriot*, August 12, 1862; *Barnstable Patriot*, October 7, 1862; Barnstable Rebellion Record, Barnstable Town Hall, Hyannis, Massachusetts; Barnstable County Probate Records for Aaron H. Young, 1862; *Barnstable Patriot*, September 16, 1862. Captain Robert B. Hallett of Hyannis purchased the mail and used it as a sutler's store boat in the South.

33. Haines Letters, August 17 and November 1, 1862; *Barnstable Patriot*, September 23, 1862; *Barnstable Patriot*, February 12, 1895.

34. *Barnstable Patriot*, June 12, 1905.

35. Thomas Wheeler Jr., National Archives Pension Records.

36. Joshua Small, National Archives Pension Records.

37. Samuel Sampson, Artemus Young, Lorenzo Drury, Eri Snow and Samuel Knowles, National Archives Pension Records.

38. Karl Marty and Lee C. Drickamer, eds., *Drummer Boy: The Civil War Diary of Edwin Hale Lincoln* (Raleigh, NC: Ivy House Publishing, 2005), 12; *Boston Daily Courier*, December 13, 1862.

39. *Barnstable Patriot*, May 6, 1862; Flint Whitlock, *Distant Bugles, Distant Drums: The Union Response to the Confederate Invasion of New Mexico* (Boulder: University Press of Colorado, 2006), 211.

40. Charles F. Herberger, ed., *A Yankee at Arms: The Diary of Lieutenant Augustus D. Ayling, Twenty-Ninth Massachusetts Volunteers* (Knoxville: University of Tennessee Press, 1999), 50–52.

41. Charles Dillingham, National Archives Service Records.

42. Charles E. Davis, *Three Years in the Army: The Story of the Thirteenth Massachusetts Volunteers* (Boston: privately printed, 1894), 108–119; *Barnstable Patriot*, September 9, 1862; Thomas Wheeler Jr., National Archives Pension Records.

43. David B. Coleman, Gilman Hook, Nathan Winslow and George N. Munsell, National Archives Pension Records.

44. Haines Letters, January 29, 1863.

45. *Yarmouth Register*, Jan 19, 1863; Horatio Lewis Journal, Chatham Historical Society, Chatham, Massachusetts; Henry Knippe, National Archives Pension Records.

46. *Barnstable Patriot*, September 9, 1862; *Barnstable Patriot*, September 30, 1862; *Barnstable Patriot*, October 14, 1862; *Cape Cod Republican*, September 25, 1862; "Ladies Aid and Soldiers Relief 1862," microfilm, GSU 124, Massachusetts State Archives, Boston, Massachusetts.

6. HOME FRONT AND FRONT LINE 1863

1. *Yarmouth Register*, January 9, 1863; George W. Powers, *The Story of the Thirty-Eighth Regiment of Massachusetts Volunteers* (Cambridge, MA: Cambridge Press, 1866), 34; *Barnstable Patriot*, January 27, 1863.
2. Albert W. Mann, *History of the Forty-fifth Regiment Massachusetts Volunteer Militia* (Boston: W. Spooner, 1908), 331; Charles R. Codman, Soldier Studies.org; Alfred C. Finney and Warren H. Ellis, National Archives Pension Records; Lewis Journal. Ellis's home was near the present-day Yarmouthport playground.
3. William H. Matthews, Samuel Knowles and Joseph N. Landers, National Archives Pension Records.
4. Benjamin Lovell and Azariah Walker, National Archives Pension Records; Edwin Bearse Letters, Massachusetts Historical Society, Boston, Massachusetts.
5. Supplement to the War of the Rebellion, vol. 29, 375 and 382; Francis Tripp, National Archives Pension Records.
6. Mann, *History of the Forty-Fifth*, 258; Haines Letters, May 13, 1863.
7. Cyrus B. Fish, National Archives Pension Records.
8. Cyrus B. Fish and Abijah Baker, National Archives Pension Records.
9. Jones Diary.
10. Cornelius B. Fish, National Archives Pension Records.
11. Augustus Foster and Elijah Swift, National Archives Service Records; Jehiel and Cornelius Fish, National Archives Pension Records.
12. Andrew P. Cobb, National Archives Pension Records; James K. Ewer, *The Third Massachusetts Cavalry in the War for the Union* (Maplewood, MA; Perry Press, 1903), 317; War of the Rebellion, series 1, vol. 26, part 1, 293.
13. Joseph Lincoln Papers, Martha Huckins letter, July 13, 1863, manuscript 3, box 1, folder 5, Sturgis Library. Barnstable, Massachusetts.
14. Francis Rogers Diary, Chatham Historical Society, Chatham, Massachusetts.
15. *Boston Daily Courier*, July 11, 1863; *Barnstable Patriot*, July 14, 1863; *Barnstable Patriot*, July 28, 1863; George Lockwood, National Archives Service Records; Rogers Diary.
16. Register of Applications of Officers of Colored Troops 1864–66, National Archives Record Group 94. Entry 369; Executive Letters.
17. Samuel T. Alton and Colin Shaw, National Archives Service Records.
18. George F.W. Haines, National Archives Service Records; Frank P. Deane, ed., *"My Dear Wife…": The Civil War Letters of David Brett, Ninth Massachusetts Battery* (N.p.: Frank Putnam Deane II, 1964), 3 and 59.
19. Bruce C. Kelley and Mark A. Snell, eds., *Bugle Resounding: Music and Musicians of the Civil War Era* (Columbia: University of Missouri Press, 2004), 218.
20. William D. Holmes Diary, Barnstable Rebellion Record, Barnstable, Massachusetts.
21. Cyrus Fish and Noah Bradford, National Archives Pension Records; *Barnstable Patriot*, October 6 and Nov 3, 1863; Holmes Diary.
22. *Barnstable Patriot*, December 8, 1863; *Barnstable Patriot*, December 22, 1863; Luther Hammond, National Archives Pension Records.
23. James H. Baker, National Archives Pension Records.

24. Descriptive Lists of Drafted Men and Substitutes, Waltham, Massachusetts, National Archives Record Group 110, entry 855, National Archives, Waltham, Massachusetts.

25. Nathan T. Jenkins, National Archives Pension Records; *Boston Daily Courier*, August 1, 1863; *Barnstable Patriot*, September 8, 1863; Holmes Diary; *Boston Daily Courier*, July 28, 1863.

26. *Boston Daily Courier*, August 21, 1863; Nathan T. Jenkins, National Archives Pension Records.

27. Charles L. Ellis, National Archives Pension Records; *Yarmouth Register*, July 11, 1862.

28. *Barnstable Patriot*, November 3, 1863; *Cape Cod Republican*, November 26, 1863; *Cape Cod Republican*, December 10, 1863; *Cape Cod Republican*, December 17, 1863; *Cape Cod Republican*, December 24, 1863.

29. Dana Eldridge, *A Cape Cod Kinship: Two Centuries, Two Wars, Two Men* (East Orleans, MA: Dana W. Eldridge, 2008), 32.

7. Home Front and Front Line, 1864-65

1. John E. Smith Diary, University of Delaware Special Collections, Newark, Delaware; *Barnstable Patriot*, January 12, 1864.

2. *Barnstable Patriot*, December 22, 1863; *Barnstable Patriot*, February 16, 1864; Executive Letters.

3. Benjamin K. Lombard, National Archives Pension Records; Record of Arrested Deserters, Waltham, Massachusetts, National Archives Record Group 110, entry 862, National Archives, Waltham, MA.

4. Simeon C. Childs Jr., National Archives Pension Records; Smith Diary.

5. *Cape Cod Republican*, March 31, 1864.

6. John E. Smith Correspondence, U.S. Army Heritage and Education Center, Carlisle, Pennsylvania; Stephen Minot Weld, *War Diary and Letters of Stephen Minot Weld 1861–1865* (Cambridge, MA: Riverside Press, 1912), 259–262; Smith Diary, March 31, 1864.

7. Stephen Minot Weld, *War Diary*, 274; Smith Diary; Joseph J. Rudolph Diary, U.S. Army Heritage and Education Center, Carlisle, Pennsylvania.

8. Smith Diary; Regimental books of the Fifty-sixth Massachusetts, vol. 2, National Archives Record Group 94, National Archives, Washington, D.C.

9. Charles W. Hamilton, Aaron Snow, John B. Tuttle and Benjamin K. Lombard, National Archives Pension Records.

10. Seth T. Howes, Stephen Smith and Timothy Taylor, National Archives Pension Records.

11. *Barnstable Patriot*, May 24, 1964; William Harley, National Archives Service Records; Barnstable County Probate Records for William Harley, 1864; Francis S. Cahoon Diary, courtesy Burton Derick, Dennis, Massachusetts.

12. Eldridge, *Cape Cod Kinship*, 84; Freeman Hall Jr., Moses Doane and Ansel L. Studley, National Archives Pension Records; *Barnstable Patriot*, May 31, 1864.

13. Aaron W. Snow, National Archives Pension Records.

14. William R. Plum, *The Military Telegraph During the Civil War in the United States*, vol. 2 (Chicago: Jansen, McClung and Company, 1882), 133.

15. Bearse Letters.

16. *Barnstable Patriot*, June 7, 1864; Holmes Diary; Bearse Letters.

17. *Barnstable Patriot*, July 5, 1864; Chatham Historical Society Civil War Records, Chatham, Massachusetts.

18. John B. Tuttle, National Archives Pension Records.

19. Stephen R. Howes, National Archives Pension and Service Records; *Barnstable Patriot*, June 21, 1864.

20. Daniel M. Hall, National Archives Pension Records.

21. Ibid.

22. James Ewer and Henry J. Besse, National Archives Pension Records.

23. Personal Papers of Medical Officers and Physicians, Box 441, National Archives Record Group 94, entry 561, National Archives, Washington, D.C.; *Barnstable Patriot*, July 26, 1864.

24. Everett Doane, National Archives Pension Records.

25. Thomas W. Jones, Noah Bradford, Jesse Pendergrast and Franklin Hammond, National Archives Pension Records; Chatham Historical Society Civil War Records.

26. Edwin S. Nickerson, National Archives Pension Records.

27. Rawlins Atkins, National Archives Pension Records.

28. James F. Schmutz, *The Battle of the Crater: A Compete History* (Jefferson, NC: McFarland and Company, 2009), 100; Stephen Minot Weld, *War Diary*, 356.

29. Schmutz, *Battle of the Crater*, 296; Pliny Freeman and Everett Doane, National Archives Pension Records. By officers, Doane may have meant Ledlie, who was drinking rum in a bombproof during the assault.

30. Elkanah Smith, National Archives Pension Records; John Romeo (Twenty-third U.S. Colored Troops), National Archives Service Records.

31. Edwin S. Nickerson, National Archives Pension Records; *Cape Cod Republican*, September 1, 1864.

32. Job and Simeon C. Childs Jr., National Archives Pension Records.

33. Samuel J. Wood, National Archives Pension Records.

34. Seth T. Howes, National Archives Pension Records

35. Benjamin H. Matthews and Benjamin Batchelder, National Archives Pension Records.

36. Ansel L. Studley, National Archives Pension and Service Records.

37. Zebina Dill, National Archives Service Records; Francis L. Doane, National Archives Pension Records; *Barnstable Patriot*, February 7, 1921; Horace Lovell, "Orange County's Reluctant Tourist," *Newsletter: Orange County Virginia Historical Society* 38, no. 1 (March 2007).

38. Louis A. Brown, *The Salisbury Prison: A Case Study of a Confederate Military Prison 1861–1865* (Wilmington, NC: Broadfoot Publishing, 1992), 134; Ezra B. Ryder, National Archives Pension Records; *Barnstable Patriot*, January 29, 1877.

39. Brown, *Salisbury Prison*, 144; *Falmouth Enterprise*, August 29, 1961; Barnabas G. Baker and Thomas B. Bourne, National Archives Pension Records.

40. Nathan Gill Diary, U.S. Army Heritage and Education Center, Carlisle, Pennsylvania.

41. David P. Ryder, National Archives Pension Records; *Barnstable Patriot*, August 22, 1865.

42. *Barnstable Patriot*, April 11, 1865; *Barnstable Patriot*, June 27, 1865; *Yarmouth Register*, July 14, 1865; Thomas M. Gibbs Letters, Bourne Historical Society, Bourne, Massachusetts.

8. Final Trumpet

1. *Barnstable Patriot*, July 30, 1850; *Barnstable Patriot*, January 5, 1864; *Barnstable Patriot*, August 9, 1864; *Barnstable Patriot*, June 18, 1872; Schouler, *History of Massachusetts in the Civil War*, Vol. 2, 31.

2. *Barnstable Patriot*, July 12, 1870.

3. *Barnstable Patriot*, September 26, 1865; *Barnstable Patriot*, May 21, 1867; *Barnstable Patriot*, June 21, 1870; *Barnstable Patriot*, July 12, 1870.

4. Simeon Cahoon, National Archives Pension Records.

5. Ibid.

6. John L.D. Hopkins, National Archives Pension Records.

7. Ibid.

8. George E. Crocker, National Archives Pension Records.

9. George E. Crocker, National Archives Service Records.

BIBLIOGRAPHY

PRIMARY SOURCES
Manuscripts

Barnstable Rebellion Record. Barnstable Town Hall. Barnstable, Massachusetts.
Charles Chipman Letters. U. S. Army Heritage and Education Center. Carlisle, Pennsylvania.
Chatham Historical Society Civil War Records. Chatham, Massachusetts.
Daniel Larned Papers. Library of Congress, Washington, D.C.
Edwin Bearse Letters. Massachusetts Historical Society. Boston, Massachusetts.
Francis Rogers Diary. Chatham Historical Society. Chatham, Massachusetts.
Francis S. Cahoon Diary. Courtesy Burton Derick, Dennis, Massachusetts.
George L. Haines Letters. Sandwich Town Archives. Sandwich, Massachusetts.
Harriet Sears Diary. Dennis Historical Society. Dennis, Massachusetts.
Horatio Lewis Journal. Chatham Historical Society. Chatham, Massachusetts.
John E. Smith Correspondence. U. S. Army Heritage and Education Center. Carlisle, Pennsylvania.
John E. Smith Diary. University of Delaware Special Collections, Newark, Delaware.
Joseph J. Rudolph Diary. U. S. Army Heritage and Education Center. Carlisle, Pennsylvania.
Joseph Lincoln Papers. Sturgis Library. Barnstable, Massachusetts.
Maria Withington Jones Diary. New Bedford Whaling Museum. New Bedford, Massachusetts.
Nathan Gill Diary. U. S. Army Heritage and Education Center. Carlisle, Massachusetts.
Parker Pillsbury Letters. Wardman Library. Whittier College. Whittier, California.
Robert B. Forbes Diary and Letters. Massachusetts History Society. Boston, Massachusetts.
Samuel F. Du Pont Correspondence. Hagley Museum and Library. Wilmington, Delaware.
Thomas Hollis Letter. Houghton Library. Harvard University, Cambridge, Massachusetts.
Thomas M. Gibbs Letters. Bourne Historical Society. Bourne, Massachusetts.
William D. Holmes Diary. Barnstable Rebellion Record. Barnstable, Massachusetts.

National Archives, Washington, D.C.

Letters Received by the Secretary of the Navy from Commanding Officers of Squadrons. Microfilm 89.
Letters Received by the Secretary of the Navy from Officers Below the Rank of Commander. Microfilm 148.

Miscellaneous Letters Received by the Secretary of the Navy. Microfilm 124.
Miscellaneous Letters Sent by the Secretary of the Navy. Microfilm 209.
Personal Papers of Medical Officers and Physicians. Record Group 94, entry 561.
Records Concerning Pilots. Record Group 45, entry 130.
Regimental Books. Record Group 94.
Register of Applications of Officers of Colored Troops 1864–66. Record Group 94, entry 369.
Vessel Files. Record Group 92, entry 1403.

National Archives, Waltham, Massachusetts

Descriptive Lists of Drafted Men and Substitutes. Record Group 110, entry 855.
Record of Arrested Deserters. Record Group 110, entry 862.

Massachusetts State Archives

Executive Letters.
"Ladies Aid and Soldiers Relief 1862." Microfilm GSU 124.
Marriage Records.

U.S. Government Records

House Executive Document no. 337. *Vessels Bought, Sold and Chartered by the United States Quartermaster.* 40th Cong., 2nd sess., 1867.
Official Records of the Union and Confederate Navies in the War of the Rebellion.
Senate Committee Reports. *Brig Sabao.* 39th Cong., 1st sess., 1865–66.
Senate Report no. 84. *Employment of Transport Vessels.* 37th Cong., 3rd sess., 1861-1863.
The War of the Rebellion: A Compilation of the Official Records of the Union and Confederate Armies.

Newspapers, Massachusetts

Barnstable Patriot
Boston Daily Advertiser
Boston Daily Courier
Boston Daily Evening Traveler
Boston Evening Journal
Cape Cod Republican (Harwich)
Falmouth Enterprise
Hyannis Patriot
Lowell Daily Citizen and News
Middleboro Gazette
New Bedford Daily Mercury
New Bedford Republican Standard
Yarmouth Register

Newspapers, non-Massachusetts

Baltimore Sun
New Orleans Times Picayune
New South
New York Herald

Bibliography

New York Times
New York Tribune
Philadelphia Inquirer
Richmond Dispatch
Washington Daily Globe

Printed Primary Source Books

Bacon, Georgeanna Woolsey. *Letters of a Family During the War, 1861-1865*, vol. 2., privately printed, 1899.

Barnstable Rebellion Record, Barnstable Town Hall, Hyannis, MA.

Bearse, Austin. *Reminiscences of Fugitive-Slave Days in Boston*. Boston: privately printed, 1880.

Davis, Charles E. *Three Years in the Army: The Story of the Thirteenth Massachusetts Volunteers*. Boston: privately printed, 1894.

Deane, Frank P., ed. *"My Dear Wife…": The Civil War Letters of David Brett, Ninth Massachusetts Battery*. N.p.: Frank Putnam Deane II, 1964.

Drickamer, Lee C., and Karl Marty, eds. *Drummer Boy: The Civil War Diary of Edwin Hale Lincoln*. Raleigh, NC: Ivy House Publishing, 2005.

Eldridge, Dana. *A Cape Cod Kinship: Two Centuries, Two Wars, Two Men*. East Orleans, MA: Dana W. Eldridge, 2008.

Ewer, James K. *The Third Massachusetts Cavalry in the War for the Union*. Maplewood, MA: Perry Press, 1903.

Forbes, Robert B. *Personal Reminiscences*. Boston: Little Brown, 1878.

Gordon, George H. *A War Diary of Events of the War of the Great Rebellion 1863–1865*. Boston: Osgood and Company, 1882.

Gray, John Chipman and John Codman Ropes. *War Letters 1862–1865*. Boston: Houghton Mifflin, 1927.

Herberger, Charles F., ed. *A Yankee at Arms: The Diary of Lieutenant Augustus D. Ayling, Twenty-Ninth Massachusetts Volunteers*. Knoxville: University of Tennessee Press, 1999.

Leonard, Andrea. *Crocker Genealogy*, vol. 2. Bowie, MD: Heritage Books, 1997.

Mann, Albert W. *History of the Forty-Fifth Regiment Massachusetts Volunteer Militia*. Boston: W. Spooner, 1908.

Nason, George W. *Minutemen of '61*. Boston: Smith and McCance, 1910.

Plum, William R. *The Military Telegraph in the Civil War*. Vol. 2. Chicago: Jansen, McClung and Company, 1882.

Powers, George W. *The Story of the Thirty-Eighth Regiment of Massachusetts Volunteers*. Cambridge, MA: Cambridge Press, 1866.

Roe, Alfred S. *The Fifth Regiment Massachusetts Volunteer Infantry*. Boston: Fifth Regiment Veterans Association, 1911.

———. *The Thirty-Ninth Regiment Massachusetts Volunteers 1862–1865*. Worcester, MA, 1914.

Weld, Stephen M. *War Diary and Letters of Stephen Minot Weld 1861–1865*. Cambridge, MA: Riverside Press, 1912.

Periodicals

Confederate Veteran
United Service Magazine

PRINTED SECONDARY SOURCES

Books

Barlow, Raymond E., and Joan E. Kaiser. *The Glass Industry in Sandwich*, vol. 3. Windham, NH: Barlow-Kaiser Barlow Publishing Co., Inc., 1983.

Brown, Louis A. *The Salisbury Prison: A Case Study of a Confederate Military Prison 1861-1865*. Wilmington, NC: Broadfoot Publishing, 1992.

Campbell, Stanley W. *The Slave Catchers: Enforcement of the Fugitive Slave Law 1850–1860*. New York: W.W. Norton Co., 1972.

Cotham, Edward T. *Battle on the Bay: The Civil War Struggle of Galveston*. Austin: University of Texas Press, 1998.

Deyo, Simeon. *History of Barnstable County*. New York: H.W. Blake, 1890.

Doane, Alfred A., comp. *The Doane Family and Their Descendants*. Boston: Alfred A. Doane, 1902.

Joiner, Gary D. *Through the Howling Wilderness: The 1864 Red River Campaign and Union Failure in the West*. Knoxville: University of Tennessee Press, 2006.

Kelley, Bruce C., and Mark A. Snell, eds. *Bugle Resounding: Music and Musicians of the Civil War Era*. Columbia: University of Missouri Press, 2004.

Massachusetts Soldiers, Sailors and Marines of the Civil War. Norwood, MA: Norwood Press, 1933.

Miller, Richard F. *Harvard's Civil War: A History of the Twentieth Massachusetts Volunteer Infantry*. Hanover, NH: University Press of New England, 2005.

Nickerson, Joseph A. Jr., and Louise D. Nickerson. *Chatham Sea Captains in the Age of Sail*. Charleston: The History Press, 2008.

O'Neil, Neva. *Master Mariners of Dennis*. Dennis, MA: Dennis Historical Society, 1965.

Palfrey, Francis W. *Memoir of William Francis Bartlett*. Cambridge: Riverside Press, 1878.

Phisterer, Frederick, comp. *New York in the War of the Rebellion 1861–1865*. Albany: Lyon Company, 1912.

Rich, Shebnah. *Truro Cape Cod or Landmarks and Seamarks*. Boston: D. Lothrop and Co., 1884.

Ringle, Dennis. *Life in Mr. Lincoln's Navy*. Annapolis: Naval Institute Press, 1998.

Robinson, William Jr. *The Confederate Privateers*. New Haven: Yale University Press, 1928.

Salerno, Beth A. *Sister Societies: Women's Antislavery Organizations in Antebellum America*. DeKalb: Northern Illinois University Press, 2005.

Schouler, William. A History of Massachusetts in the Civil War. Two Vols. Boston: E.P. Dutton and Co., 1868.

Sears, J. Henry. *Brewster Shipmasters*. Yarmouthport, MA: C.W. Swift, 1906.

Silverstone, Paul H. *Civil War Navies 1855–1883*. Annapolis: Naval Institute Press, 2001.

Whitlock, Flint. *Distant Bugles, Distant Drums: The Union Response to the Confederate Invasion of New Mexico*. Boulder: University Press of Colorado, 2006.

Periodicals

Civil War History
Massachusetts Historical Review
New England Quarterly

INDEX

A

Abaellino (ship) 31
Abby Bradford (schooner) 32
Abby Bursley (schooner) 51
Acorn (brig) 17
Alexandria, Louisiana 52
Alexandria, Virginia 72, 89,
    105
Allen, Jesse 55
Alton
  Joseph 81
  Samuel T. 81
Amazonian (ship) 52
Ames, Cephas I. 17–18
Andersonville, Georgia 101
Andrew, Governor John 27,
    35–36, 66–67, 84
Arey, Elbridge 51
Armstrong, Francis 93
Atkins
  James P. 93–94
  Joshua Jr. 23
  Rawlins T. 28, 33, 84–86,
    97
Atlantic Messenger 21
Atlantic (steamer) 48
Atwood
  Hawes Jr. 28, 41
  John W. 74, 80
  Nathaniel E. 59

Avon (schooner) 51
Ayling, Augustus D. 72

B

Backus
  George H. 38
  Simeon 32
Bacon
  Edward B. 21
  George W. 40
  Nathaniel 50
  Onan 27
Baker
  Abijah 77
  Barnabas G. 102
  Charles G. 41, 55
  Charles P. 66
  Clara 80
  Darius 66
  David H. 41
  Elnathan 82
  Henry B. 100
  James H. 82
  James M. 55, 58
  Levi 20
  Oliver 51
Balls Bluff, Virginia 54
Banks Expedition 66
Banks, General Nathaniel
    51–52, 78, 94

Barnstable Academy 105
Barnstable County Antislavery
    Society 16
Barnstable Female Antislavery
    Society 12
Barnstable Patriot 7, 11, 16,
    18–20, 22, 25, 29,
    37–38, 40, 53, 82, 85,
    103–104
Barnstable Village Ladies
    Relief Society 53,
    105
Barnstable Village,
    Massachusetts 15,
    19, 23, 35, 52, 58, 63,
    69, 92, 106
Bassett
  Benjamin 93
  Clarence 74
  Joseph 70, 76
  William H. 67
Batchelder, Benjamin 63,
    101
Baxter
  Benjamin D. 46
  Edwin 49, 50, 52
  Horatio N. 33
  Joseph 40
  Rodney 24, 25, 27, 33, 52,
    67, 69
  Samuel S. 26, 48, 50

Bearse
  Alonzo 70
  Austin 14, 17–18
  Charles C. 15
  Edwin 76, 92–93
  George H. 75
  Harrison 49
  Olive 14
  Owen 44
  Patience 53
  William 48
Beaufort, North Carolina 50
Bee, Benjamin 48
Benjamin Deford (steamer) 40, 44, 48, 50
Benjamin Delano (brig) 49, 52
Bennett, Jeremiah 93–94
Benson, Henry 74
Berlin, Maryland 82
Berry, Abraham 83
Berry, Horace N. 52
Besse
  Henry 95
  Willard 95
Birmingham, England 54
Blackburn's Ford, Virginia 33
Black Swan (schooner) 99
Blagden, James 93
Blake
  David 58
  Hannah 58
Blauvelt, James 63
Bloomer, Joseph 63
Bodfish, John 40
Bolton, John 93
Boston and Sandwich
    Glassworks 29
Boston Committee of
    Vigilance 17
Bourne
  Henry 50, 102
  Thomas B. 101–102
Bowman, Benjamin 62
Bradford, Noah 82, 96
Branch, William 83
Brashear City, Louisiana 78
Brazos Santiago, Texas 52
Breckenridge, John 19, 23

Brewster, Massachusetts 17, 29, 49, 60, 67, 79
Bride (packet) 29
Briggs, Seth 29
Brooks, Sidney 99–100
Brown
  John 22
  Thaddeus 39
  William W. 13, 15
Buchanan, President James 18–20, 24
Bull Run, Virginia 34, 72
Burgess
  Howard 28
  James F. 51
Burleigh, C.M. 13
Burlingame, Pardon 44
Burnside Expedition 41, 45, 55, 59
Burnside, General Ambrose 41, 46, 86, 88–89, 97
Bursley, Ira 27
Burt, Jonathan 48
Butler Expedition 47
Butler, General Benjamin 47, 50

C

Cahoon
  Elizabeth 106
  Ellen 68
  Francis S. 90
  Obed 82
  Sally 101
  Simeon 106–107
  Stephen 106–107
Calhoun, CSS (privateer) 31
Cambridge (steamer) 29, 54
Camp Lander, Massachusetts 67
Camp Stanton, Massachusetts 61–64
Cape Henlopen, Delaware 31
Cash, Freeman 76
Cass, Senator Lewis 15
Cavendy, Captain Edward 39

Cedar Creek, Virginia 101, 102
Cedar Mountain, Virginia 72
Centerville Female
    Antislavery Society 14
Centerville, Massachusetts 13, 18, 32, 73
Chamberlain
  Allen T. 52, 106
  Betsey 105
  Eliza A. 105–106
  Joshua 105
Charmer (schooner) 44
Chase
  Braddock 48, 58
  Kelly 93
  Lawrence 66
  Luke B. 32, 36, 41
Chatham, Massachusetts 13–14, 23, 30, 48, 53, 60, 63, 80, 84–85, 96
Chelsea, Massachusetts 33, 72
Chesapeake (steamer) 44
Childs
  George W. 93
  Job 99–100
  Simeon C. Jr. 86, 88, 99
Chipman
  Charles 29, 58
  William H. 41
City of Bath (propeller) 49
City of New York (propeller) 45
City Point, Virginia 27
Clark, George W. 84
Cobb
  Alfred S. 71
  Andrew P. 65, 79
  Freeman 59
Codman, Colonel Charles R. 69, 75
Cold Harbor, Virginia 93, 95
Coleman
  David 73
  Thomas Jr. 86
Collins, Isaac 29
Commodore Hull, USS 48
Concord, Massachusetts 27

Conquest (transport) 47
Constitution (steamer) 47, 58
Convoy (transport) 80
Cook
  Barnabas 102
  David E. 55
  Lemuel 40
Coombs
  Edwin 21
  Henry 17, 22
Cotuit, Massachusetts 44, 69
Cowan, John H. 83, 89
Crocker
  Asa 58
  Benjamin Jr. 51
  Charles W. 63, 83
  Enoch 34
  George E. 108
  Horace 58
  Temperance 58
  Thomas F. 83
Crosby
  Elkanah 28
  Lewis 32
Crowell
  Arthur 33
  David 63
  Davis 40
  Ebenezer 39, 52
  Ephraim 32
  Ezra 30
  George H. 44
  George W. 51
  Gorham 21
  Higgins 52, 79
  Isaac B. 72–73
  John 48
  Philander Jr. 33
  Prince S. 16
  Sidney 44
  Simeon 41
Cushing, Caleb 21
C.W. Thomas (steamer) 50–51

D

Daniel Webster (bark) 48
Danville, Virginia 101
David Howes (schooner) 106

Davis
  Benjamin 54
  Henry O. 78
  President Jefferson 30, 35
  Thomas 54, 73
Dawn (bark) 36
Day
  Elizabeth 105
  Joseph M. 63–64
Dean, Cornelius 65
DeMolay (steamer) 40, 83
Dennis, Massachusetts
    13–14, 23, 61
Dennisport, Massachusetts
    76
Denver, Colorado Territory
    71
Dill
  Theophilus 65
  Zebina 92, 101
Dillingham
  Charles 72
Dixon, William 92, 101
Doane
  Abiathur 49
  Catherine H. 17
  Daniel 33
  Edwin 51
  Eliphalet 69
  Everett 95, 99
  Francis L. 101
  Henry 67–68, 80
  Kies 17
  Moses 92
  Solomon 101
Donaldson, Hugh G. 99
Doty, Leonard 31, 62
Drewry's Bluff, Virginia 92
Drury, Lorenzo
    70
Dudley, Albion S.
    28
Dudley Buck (steamer) 50
Dunn, Mary 23
Du Pont, Samuel 48
Duruin, I.S. 34
Dyer, Paul 40

E

East Dennis, Massachusetts
    22, 55, 62, 74
East Falmouth, Massachusetts
    60, 78, 82
Eastham, Massachusetts 12,
    20, 55, 67, 99
East Harwich, Massachusetts
    63, 106, 107
Eldridge
  Ebenezer 66, 90
  Joshua H. 31–32
  Kimball 17
  Nathan 90
  Oliver 27–28
  Prince 63
  Susan 31
  Thomas 66
  Ward 33, 45
  Washington 89
Eldridge's Hotel 64, 69
Eleventh Massachusetts
    Regiment 81
Elisha Doane (brig) 31
Elizabeth B. (schooner) 21
Ellis
  Charles L. 83–84
  Daniel 63
  Warren H. 75
El Paso, Texas 25
E.M. Dyer (schooner) 50
Emory, General 78
Empire City (steamer) 26, 39,
    44, 48, 49, 52
E. Nickerson (schooner) 51
Evans, William 40
Ewer
  Benjamin 55
  Henry Jr. 55
  James B. Jr. 65, 94
Exact (steamer) 52, 79

F

Fairhaven, Connecticut 101
Fall River, Massachusetts 27
Falmouth, Massachusetts 13,
    17, 29–30, 53, 62, 75
Fannie Currie (schooner) 49

Field, William 63, 103
Fifteenth Massachusetts
    Regiment 89
Fifth Massachusetts Light
    Artillery 81
Fifth Massachusetts Regiment
    28, 66–67, 71, 74–76,
    79
Fifty-eighth Massachusetts
    Regiment 85–90,
    96–98, 103–104, 107
Fifty-fifth Massachusetts
    Regiment 83
Fifty-fourth Massachusetts
    Regiment 40, 80,
    83, 95
Fifty-sixth Massachusetts
    Regiment 85, 85–89,
    93, 97–99
Fifty-sixth Ohio Regiment 52
Fillmore, Millard 15, 19
Finney
    Alfred 66, 75
    Charles 66, 75
First Maine Cavalry 58
First Massachusetts Regiment
    33, 84
First Regiment Colorado
    Volunteers 71
First Vermont Battery 52
Fish
    Alvin 62
    Cornelius B. 78
    Cyrus 63, 77, 82, 92
    Jehiel 78
    John F. 55
    Obed M. 95
    Pamelia 78
    Rufus 62
Fishing bounty 38–39
Forbes, Robert B. 35–36, 40
Forest City (schooner) 49
Fort Fisher, North Carolina
    51
Fortieth Massachusetts
    Regiment 49–51,
    64–65, 70, 77, 82–83,
    92, 100–101
Fort Lafayette, New York 44

Fort Warren, Massachusetts
    45–46
Forty-eighth Pennsylvania
    Regiment 97
Forty-fifth Massachusetts
    Regiment 69, 74–77
Forty-first Massachusetts
    Regiment 52, 65,
    65–66, 76, 79, 85
Forty-seventh Massachusetts
    Regiment 52, 69–71,
    75–76
Forty-third Massachusetts
    Regiment 67, 70,
    74–76, 80, 90
Foster
    Augustus 78
    Daniel 17–18
    John G. 74
    Josiah 69
    Stephen S. 15
Fourteenth Massachusetts
    Battery 86, 88, 99
Fourth Massachusetts
    Regiment 27
Fox, Assistant Secretary 38
Fredericksburg, Virginia 27,
    54, 92, 101
Freeman
    Ezra 32
    George H. 28
    Hartwell 64, 80
    Jesse Jr. 88
    Josiah 40
    Josiah C. 83
    Pliny 98
    Reverend Frederick 64
Free Soil Party 15–16, 18
Fremont, John C. 18–20
French, Reverend Edward
    53, 63

G

Galveston, Texas 31, 33
Garrison, William H. 83
Garrison, William L. 11,
    12, 16
Gemsbok (bark) 36, 38
George G. Baker (schooner) 33

George Shattuck (steamer) 83
Gettysburg, Pennsylvania
    80–82, 84
Gibbs
    Ann Maria 104
    Thomas 104
Gifford, William 82, 92
Gill, Nathan A. 62, 103
Glendale, Virginia 72–73
Glorieta Pass, New Mexico
    Territory 71
Godfrey, John W. 39–40
Goldsboro, North Carolina
    74
Gordon, General George 49
Gould, William A. 63
Grant, General U.S. 50, 78,
    88, 90, 92–93, 95–96
Greenleaf, John W. 67
Guide (steamer) 50–51

H

Haffords, William 39–40
Haines
    George F.W. 81
    George L. 66, 69, 77
    James G.B. 64
Halifax, Nova Scotia 32
Hall
    Charles B. 69
    Cordelia 74
    Daniel M. 94
    Freeman Jr. 90
    Jeremiah 67
    John T. 31
    Joseph 67
    Joseph R. 86
    William C. 34, 92
Hallett
    Benjamin F. 18
    George H. 23
    Joshua 40
    William A. 40
Hamblin, Lloyd B.
    41
Hamilton, Charles W. 84, 89
Hamlin, Benjamin 72
Hammond, Franklin 80,
    96–97

Handy
Luther 40
Moses 101
Harding
David J. 52
Hannah 92, 96
Samuel 92, 96
Samuel G. 48
Theophilus 83
Hardy
Alpheus 44, 47–48, 63
Thomas C. 40
Harley, William 80, 87, 90
Harper, William H. 64–65
Harwich, Massachusetts
13–17, 30, 85
Harwichport, Massachusetts
30, 33, 51
Hatch, Freeman 102
Hatteras, North Carolina
32–33, 45, 49
Havana, Cuba 48
Heald, James H. 72
Hebard, Reverend Frederick
53
Heffernan, Edward 65
Herbert Manton (schooner) 32
Hewins, William 78
Higgins, Atkins 55
Hilton Head, South
Carolina 70
Hinckley
Eli 17
Francis 21
Louise 21
Nathaniel 15
Holley, Sally 21
Hollis, Thomas 54, 73
Holmes
Charles 99
Oliver 58
William D. 82
Holway
Edward 83–84
Joseph 82
Hooker, Joseph 77
Hook, Gilman 73, 76
Hooten, Robert 88

Hopkins
Isaac 107
John L.D. 107–108
Ruth D. 107
Sylvanus 55
Howard, Colonel William
A. 41
Howard (schooner) 49
Howes
Alvan 14, 16, 22–23
Daniel 50
Elisha 26–27, 77
Elizabeth 100
Lydia 74
Mercy P. 22–23
Nancy L. 22
Samuel 100
Seth 63, 89, 100
Solomon 23, 27, 46
Stephen 93
Stephen R. 93
Huckins, Martha 79–80
Hughes
Hezekiah 76
Hurlbert, Dr. Chauncey 62
Hyannis Antislavery Society
17
Hyannis, Massachusetts 13,
14, 63, 66, 83
Hyannisport, Massachusetts
32

I

Idaho (ship) 48
Indianola, Texas 26, 52
Island City (bark) 45, 46
Ivy (privateer) 31

J

Jamestown, CSS 41
Jenkins, Nathan 83
Jerauld, Ensign 106
John Adams (whaler) 31
John Rice (steamer) 50–51
Johnson, President Andrew
52
John Warner (steamer) 52

Jones
Asa S. 63, 80
Columbus 21
Love 80
Maria W. 78
Stephen 82
Thomas 96
Joseph Whitney (steamer) 25
Julia Ford (brig) 49
Julia Smith (schooner) 50

K

Kelley
David N. 45, 51
Ezra 83
Fernandus 46
Hannah 73
Watson B. 30
Kendrick
David 103
Key West, Florida 25, 28
King, Joseph 88
Kinston, North Carolina 74
Knippe, Henry 74
Knowles
Adaline 80
Alfred 80
Samuel 70, 76
William W. 60
Knox
Thomas P. 18

L

Landers
Johm B. 34
Joseph N. 76
Lawrence, Albert H. 83
Ledlie, General James 97
Leonard, Dr. Jonathan 54
Lewis
Enoch 18
Ephraim 40
Horatio 74, 84–85
James M. 78
Julia C 14
Orrin 31
Roland 64
Sarah C. 75
Starks W. 44
Thomas C. 44

Liberator 11, 14
Liberty, Mississippi 79
Lincoln
  Abraham 23, 27, 60, 88
  Edwin H. 66–67, 71
  Jarius 66
Linnell
  Shubael 102
Little, Charles 104
Lombard
  Benjamin K. 86, 89
  Israel 35
  Sarah C. 86
Loper, R.L. 52
Loring, George 31
Lothrop
  Ansel D. 15
  Reverend Davis 16
Loveland
  Benjamin S. 54
  Winslow 25
Lovell
  Benjamin 70, 76
  Cornelius 22
  Howard H.P. 101
  Nancy 22
Lumbert, William 63
Lyman
  Charles H. 55
  Storrs 55
Lynnfield, Massachusetts
  61, 63

M

Maggi, Colonel 61
Mail (schooner) 69
Maker, Samuel 89
Mallows
  Henry 102
M. and J.C. Gilmore (brig) 17
Marchant, Allen 86
Mariner (privateer) 33
Marlboro, Massachusetts 72
Marston
  Benjamin 30
  George 35
  Russell 17, 18, 22, 64
Marstons Mills, Massachusetts
  17, 30, 33, 69, 82, 86

Mason, James 59
Massachusetts (steamer) 33,
  38
Matthews
  Benjamin H. 101–102
  Edmund 67
  Seleck H. 29
  William H. 76
Mayo
  David E. 52
  J.C. 14
  Simeon 36
May, Samuel 16
McClellan, General George
  46, 60, 71–72, 77
McKenna, Peter 54
McKowen, James 65, 102
McPherson, James B. 55
Megathlin, Captain 20
Mercy A. Howes (schooner)
  100
Mermaid (schooner) 31
Merrimac, CSS 40–41
Midnight, USS 36
Miner's Hill, Virginia
  70–71, 77
Mississippi (steamer) 39, 52,
  67, 69, 75
Modena (bark) 25
Monitor, USS 40
Monohansett (steamer) 78
Moody, Loring 16, 18
Morehead City, North
  Carolina 50
Morrill, Charles 48
Mosby's Rangers 94
Mosquito Inlet, Florida 31
Mountain Avenue (schooner)
  47
Mount Washington, USS 40
Mount Zion Freedman's
  School 105
Mullett, Charles 93
Munsell
  Dr. George N. 62, 73
  Reverend Joseph R. 22
Murphy, Terrence 54

Myrick
  George 66
  Isaac 66
  Joshua 30, 31
Mystic (brig) 52

N

Nansemond River 40, 77
Nathaniel Chase (schooner) 33
Nauset Hotel 67
New Bedford, Massachusetts
  20, 29, 44, 62, 78
New Bern, North Carolina
  32–33, 50, 74–77,
  80
Newcomb, Captain
  Valentine 62
New England Guards
  54–56
New Haven, Connecticut
  101
New York Marine Artillery
  41
Nichols, Ebenezer 32
Nicholson, John A. 89
Nickerson
  Allen 49
  Cyrus 27
  Edwin 96–97, 99
  Frederick 40
  George H. 68, 80
  George W. 106–107
  Holmes 40
  Seth 86
  Winsor 82
Ninth Massachusetts Light
  Artillery 81
Norris, Bradford 39–40
North Chatham,
  Massachusetts 63,
  96
North Dennis, Massachusetts
  13
North Harwich,
  Massachusetts 101
North Sandwich,
  Massachusetts 29,
  58, 100
North Star (steamer) 52

Nueces (bark) 32
Nuestra Señora de Regla
(steamer) 48
Nye, Joseph W. 33, 45
Nymphas C. Hall (schooner)
20

O

Ocean Pearl (ship) 48
169th New York Regiment
51
O'Neil, James 90–91
Orlando, John 21, 50
Osterville, Massachusetts
18, 32, 49, 105
Otis
Samuel 82, 92
Solomon 92

P

Pacific Mill 60
Packard
Charles M. 28
Page, William 55
Paine
Amasa 22
E. Dexter 66
John A. 49
Joseph 80
Joseph W. 28, 68
Paron C. 29, 33
Philander 16
Thomas 51
Panama (whaler) 31
Parker
D.F.W. 23, 39
James N. 31, 62
Josiah C. 40
Pease
Giles M. 80, 95
Reverend Giles 13
Pendergrast, Jesse 96
Pennsylvania Freedman's
Relief Association
105
Petersburg, Virginia 96,
99–101, 107
Pettes, Samuel 88

Phillips, William T. 33
Phinney
Eliza 53
Sylvanus 16, 19, 21, 23,
25, 29, 38, 40, 43,
59, 103
Sylvester O. 28
William W. 28
Pierce, Eliza A. 101
Pillsbury, Parker 13, 14,
15, 18
Pioneer (gunboat) 41, 55
Pitcher, Nathan 82
Plymouth, North Carolina
95
Pocasset, Massachusetts 29,
58, 60, 104
Porter, Commodore David
37
Port Hudson, Louisiana
77–79
Port Royal, South Carolina
44, 48–50
Portsmouth, New
Hampshire 41
Potomska (steamer) 32, 44, 45
Powers, John 76
Provincetown Banner 21
Provincetown Ladies Relief
Society 87
Provincetown, Massachusetts
12, 20, 35, 52, 59,
69, 85–87, 105, 108
Putnam, Caroline 21

Q

Quantrill's Raiders 94

R

Ranger (steamer) 50–51
R.B. Forbes, USS 39
Readville, Massachusetts 69,
85–86
Reindeer (schooner) 44
Remond, C.L. 13
Rich, Lyman B, 50
Rider, Godfrey Jr.
37, 61, 83

Riley, Phillip 54–55
Robbins
Gustavus C. 83
Joshua H. 16, 22
Robertville, South Carolina
103
Robinson Mill 60
Robinson, Prince
95
Rockland (steamer) 50
Rodman, William 62
Rogers
Alonzo Jr. 89
Francis 80
Roleson (brig) 21
Romeo
John 99
Rudolph, Joseph J. 89
Ryder
Alvah 63
Amos 93
David P. 89, 92, 103
Ezra B. 90, 102
John E. 70, 76
John J. 62
Kimball 25
Richard 48
Stephen A. 29

S

Sabao (brig) 41
Sabine Pass, Texas 52, 79
Sabine, USS 39
Sachem, USS 79
S.A. Hammond (schooner) 51
Salisbury, North Carolina
101–102, 107
Sampson, Samuel 70
Sandwich Guards 29
Sandwich, Massachusetts
12–14, 16, 23, 58,
60
Sandwich Observer 13
Sandy Hook 50
San Jacinto (frigate) 59
Satilla River 31
Satilla (schooner) 31
Savage's Station, Virginia
55, 72

Schamyl (bark) 98
Scudder, Mary F. 53
Sears
 Cyrus A. 69
 Elisha 49
 Harriet 22
 Winthrop 47
Second Massachusetts
  Cavalry 94
Second Massachusetts Heavy
  Artillery 80, 95
Second Massachusetts
  Regiment 72, 80, 94
Shaw, Colin 81
Ship Island, Mississippi
  47–48, 59, 75
Shiverick
 Andrew 78
 Andrew T. 77–78
 Celia 78
Shove, Dr. George 37
Sims, Thomas 17, 18
Sixteenth Massachusetts
  Regiment 55
Sixth U.S. Colored Troops
  80
Slidell, John 59
Small
 James 20
 John W. 77
 Joshua 70
 Taylor Jr. 88, 99
 Thomas 63
 Zebina H. 15
Smalley
 Ebenezer 84, 90, 96
 Henry 63
Smith
 Caleb 69
 Dr. John M. 63
 Eben S. 59
 Eliza J. 90
 Elkanah 99
 Gilbert 16, 18
 Henry A.F. 83
 Isaac Y. 74
 John E. 85–89, 99
 Josephine 108
 Mary Ann 18

Nathaniel 85, 93
Rufus 63
Samuel 16, 22
Stephen 89
Snaggy Point, Louisiana 94
Snow
 Aaron 89, 92
 Charles H. 83
 Chester 59
 David (Orleans) 35, 48
 David (Yarmouth) 66
 Eri M. 63, 70
 Josiah Jr. 48
 Laban Jr. 15
 Rebecca 92
 Stillman 15
 Zoeth, Jr. 60, 67
Soldiers Rest 105
Somerville Guards 28
Soper, Robert 31
South Carolina (steamer) 24,
  27, 33, 39, 52
South Dennis, Massachusetts
  14, 40, 46, 62, 101
South Sandwich,
  Massachusetts 55
South Yarmouth 20
Sparrow
 Benjamin C. 55, 72
 Thomas 48
 William E. 74
Spencer, Roland 63
Spotsylvania, Virginia 90,
  92, 93
Sprague, Francis W. 22
Sprightling Sea (schooner) 30
S.R. Spaulding (steamer) 23,
  27, 33, 44, 46, 49,
  51–52
Star of the West (steamer) 26,
  52, 77
State of Maine (steamer) 27–28
Steele, Danforth 107
Stevenson, Colonel Thomas
  55
Stewart, Reverend W. H. 22
Stone
 Jeremiah 15, 108
 Lucy 15

Studley
 Ansel 92, 101
 George S. 92
Sumter, CSS (raider) 32
"Swamp Angel" 49
Swift 65
 Charles 19, 23
 Elijah 31, 62, 78–79
 George W. 101–103
 Oliver 31

T

Tacony, CSS (raider) 32
Tallahassee, CSS (raider) 100
Tallahatchie River 77
Tar River 76
Taylor
 Levi 99
 Timothy 89
 Zachary 15, 16
Terror (clipper) 58
Thacher
 Ezekiel 14, 16
 Franklin 66
Thames (steamer) 51
Third Massachusetts Cavalry
  85, 94
Third Massachusetts
  Regiment 27
Thirteenth Massachusetts
  Regiment 58
Thirtieth Massachusetts
  Regiment 48
Thirty-eighth Massachusetts
  Regiment 52, 62, 66,
  75, 78, 82, 104
Thirty-fifth, Massachusetts
  Regiment 62, 65,
  73, 76
Thirty-ninth Massachusetts
  Regiment 63, 65, 80,
  101, 103
Thirty-sixth Massachusetts
  Regiment 92
Thirty-third Massachusetts
  Regiment 61, 62, 65,
  70, 83, 103
Thomas W. House (bark) 48
Tillie (steamer) 50, 102

Tinkham
Eliza 58
Martin S. 58
Richard 58
Trent (steamer) 59
Tripp, Francis 76–77
Truro, Massachusetts 12,
20, 29, 76, 86–87,
107
Tupper
William E. 41
Tuttle
John B. 80, 89, 93
Twelfth Massachusetts
Regiment 89
Twentieth Massachusetts
Regiment 54
Twenty-eighth Wisconsin
Regiment 78
Twenty-fourth Massachusetts
Regiment 54, 59, 96
Twenty-ninth Massachusetts
Regiment 55,
72–73, 108
Twiss, Alfred 62

U

Underground Railroad 22
Upham
Charles 53, 67, 80, 84–85,
89–90, 93

V

Van Buren, President Martin
15
Vicksburg, Mississippi 77,
78, 84
Vidette (gunboat) 41
Virginia Price (schooner) 48
Vitula (ship) 27

W

Wabash, USS 50
Walker, Azariah 70, 76
Waquoit, Massachusetts 48,
60, 102
Washburn, George W. 28

Washburn, William S. 55
Washington, D.C. 28, 33,
34, 44, 50, 51, 59,
62, 65, 84, 92, 105
Washington, North Carolina
76
Webster, Daniel 18
Weeks
Eunice 58
John 58
Olivia 74
Willard 58
Willard Jr. 58
Weld, Colonel 87–89
Welles, Gideon 30, 36
Wellfleet, Massachusetts
12, 20, 28, 30, 68,
87, 94
West Barnstable,
Massachusetts 18,
30, 58
West Chatham,
Massachusetts 53
West Dennis, Massachusetts
30
Western Star (schooner) 44
Western World, USS 40
West Harwich,
Massachusetts 29,
52, 90
West Point, Virginia 61, 77
West Sandwich 70, 74
West Yarmouth,
Massachusetts 21,
52
Wheeler, Thomas Jr. 70,
72–73
White, George 37
White Hall, North Carolina
74
White House Hotel 84
Wide-awakes 23
Wilderness, Virginia 89–90,
100, 107
Wild Gazelle (bark) 48
William Jenkins (steamer) 23
Wilmington, North Carolina
102, 103

Wilson, Senator Henry 27,
38
Windermere (ship) 52
Wing, Stephen 74
Winslow
Edward 59
Nathan 73
Winslow (privateer) 32
Wixon
Amos 93
Benjamin 92
Wood
Phebe 58
Samuel 100
William H. 58
Woods Hole, Massachusetts
28, 55, 95
Woodward, Ezekiel 54
Wright, Eliza 82
W.R. Newcomb (schooner) 27
Wyandotte, USS 40

Y

Yarmouth, Massachusetts
12, 16, 75, 100
Yarmouthport,
Massachusetts 14,
17, 34, 63, 66, 70,
79, 83
Yarmouth Register 10–13,
21, 72
York, CSS (privateer) 33, 44
Young
Aaron H. 69, 74
Artemus 70
David 89
Young Turk (bark) 48